THE BEAUTIFUL WARRIORS

Technofeminist Praxis in the
Twenty-First Century

Edited by Cornelia Sollfrank

The Beautiful Warriors. Technofeminist Praxis in the Twenty-First Century
Edited by Cornelia Sollfrank

ISBN 978-1-570-27-365-0

Cover design by Cornelia Sollfrank and Janine Sack, based on a visual from the
performance *À la recherche de l'information perdue* (Sollfrank, 2018)
Interior layout by Margaret Killjoy

Released by Minor Compositions 2020
Colchester / New York / Port Watson

Minor Compositions is a series of interventions & provocations drawing from
autonomous politics, avant-garde aesthetics, and the revolutions of everyday life.

Minor Compositions is an imprint of Autonomedia
www.minorcompositions.info | minorcompositions@gmail.com

Distributed by Autonomedia
PO Box 568 Williamsburgh Station
Brooklyn, NY 11211

www.autonomedia.org
info@autonomedia.org

CONTENTS

PREFACE

Cornelia Sollfrank

Translated by Valentine A. Pakis

"We have to become practiced in warfare. That means nothing less than fighting for certain worlds and against others – for particular ways of living and being in the world, and not others. And this is exactly what it means to revolt. To be for certain things and against others is a sort of "war of the worlds," but it is war as part of a proposition for peace, a proposition that is not without danger. [...] We are still able to change things, but the time to act is short. And we will know all too soon whether there can be peace at all."
— Donna Haraway

"There's no need to fear or hope, but only to look for new weapons."
— Gilles Deleuze

1

"Men and things exchange properties and
replace one another; this is what gives
technological projects their full savor."
—Bruno Latour

"The new planetary consciousness will
have to rethink machinism."
— Félix Guattari

"Pick up again the long struggle against
lofty and privileged abstraction. Perhaps
this is the core of revolutionary process."
— Adrienne Rich

WHAT RELATION DO TECHNOLOGY AND GENDER HAVE WITH ONE AN-
other? How are they mutually produced in ever-new configurations?
Can they even be thought of as two separate categories? And is it not
necessary to bring a series of additional agents into play in order to
provide a more complete picture?

This volume brings together a selection of current technofeminist
positions from the fields of art and activism. Since the cyberfeminism
of the 1990s, new ways of thinking and acting have proliferated, often as a reaction to new forms and dimensions of exploitation and
discrimination. Issues have expanded from a purely informational dimension and its emancipatory potential into a material dimension.
Questions of technology are now bound together with questions of
ecology and the economy. Online and offline are no longer separate
spheres, but have rather become a single continuum. Art may function symbolically with images, metaphors, and narratives, but it also
crosses and partially obscures the limits of activism. For its part, activism is an expression of protest against technocapitalist excess – it is an
effort to pursue new tools, instruments, and places to enable common
activity, common learning, and common unlearning. Despite the
great variety of existing positions, there is nevertheless something that
binds them together; they all negotiate gender politics with reference
to technology, and they all understand their praxis as an invitation to
take up their social and aesthetic interventions, to carry on, and never

give up. Those involved are diverse: activists and collectives working under pseudonyms, but also artists and other producers of knowledge both within and outside of academic disciplines. Their practices are networked, but often in the stratified, parallel universes of international art scenes, academic theory and research (primarily in the global North), political activism (primarily in the global South), and the techno-underground. To gather such diverse views into a single volume is to traverse many territories and cross many borders – all to pursue the possibility of thinking and acting in common.

The term *technofeminism* serves to designate these diverse practices but also – through their proximity in this book – to bring them into contact and encourage exchange. Coined in Judy Wajcman's book of the same name,[1] the concept denotes speculative and queer positions that – both in theory and in practice – question the coded relation between gender and technology. Wajcman locates technofeminism at the intersection of science and technology studies (STS) and feminist technology studies. In particular, technofeminism is interested in examining how gender relations and the hierarchy of sexual difference influence scientific research and technological innovation and how the latter, in turn, influence the constitution of gender. Translated into technofeminist practices in everyday life, this means no less than struggling for a more just and livable world for everyone in today's technoscientific culture.

Throughout, Donna Haraway looms in the background. More than 30 years ago, we learned from her that there is hardly any chance of living outside of technologies – this was not something that she lamented but, on the contrary, always understood as an opportunity. Accordingly, her feminist critique of the technosciences did not lead to an anti-scientific or technophobic attitude. Rather, it called for a more comprehensive, robust, and true science; a science with clear points of view; and a reconceptualization of science and technology to serve emancipatory ends. Haraway made essential contributions to the deconstruction of scientific knowledge as historically patriarchal, and she demonstrated that science and technology are closely linked to capitalism, militarism, colonialism, and racism. At the heart of her anti-essentialist approach is the critique of the alleged objectivity of scientific knowledge. Instead of understanding science

---

1   Judy Wajcman, *TechnoFeminism* (Cambridge, UK: Polity, 2004).

as disembodied truth, Haraway stresses its social aspects, including its potential to create narratives. According to Judy Wajcman, "For Haraway science is culture in an unprecedented sense. Her central concern is to expose the "god trick," the dominant view of science as a rational, universal, objective, non-tropic system of knowledge."[2] This entails questioning dichotomous categories such as science/ideology, nature/culture, mind/body, reason/emotion, objectivity/ subjectivity, human/machine, and physical/metaphysical on the basis of their inherent hierarchical functions. Especially relevant for technofeminist thinking is Haraway's deconstruction of the "natural" as a cultural praxis. Her concept of "situated knowledge" can be regarded as a feminist epistemology that recognizes its own contingent and localized foundations, as well as the contingent and localized foundations of other forms of knowledge. Haraway's concept of the cyborg offered a concrete conceptual tool for rethinking socialist-feminist politics in the age of technosciences.[3] It became an icon for the dissolving borders between the biological and the cultural, between the human and the machine, and thus a symbol for the queering of old dichotomies, for it was only beyond previously conceived boundaries that new forms of social and political praxis would be possible. The artificiality of corporality, the collective nature of the cyborg's subjectivity, and its inherent politics of interconnectivity were essential inspirations for cyberfeminism.[4]

The conditions of digital, networked technologies inspired the cyberfeminism of the 1990s and fuelled it to proclaim undreamt-of techno-hybrid identities and thus to evoke a new and intimate relationship between women and technology. Subsequent criticism of the dangerous essentialism of the early approaches by Sadie Plant and the VNS Matrix or of the insufficient political self-identification of the Old Boys Network fail to recognize just how effective the concept

2   Ibid., 83.

3   Donna Haraway, "A Cyborg Manifesto: Science, Technology, and Socialist-Feminism in the Late Twentieth Century," in *Simians, Cyborgs, and Women: The Reinvention of Nature*, by Haraway (New York: Routledge, 1991), 149-181.

4   See Karin Harrasser, "Herkünfte und Milieus der Cyborg," in *Die Untoten: Life Sciences & Pulp Fiction* (Hamburg: Kampnagel, 2011), http://www.untot.info/65-0-Karin-Harrasser-Herkuenfte-und-Milieus-der-Cyborgs.html (accessed August 23, 2018).

and the (political) imaginaries associated with it actually were,[5] even though (or perhaps because) it kept away from any simplistic understanding of politics but instead pulled out all the stops for queering. There was never *a* cyberfeminism or *the* cyberfeminism but rather a multitude of feminist, techno-utopian visions from a variety of disciplines and with a wide range of content, and these visions found a platform with the Old Boys Network, where they could become visible and develop in proximity to one another.[6] After OBN discontinued its activities in 2001, there was no longer an overarching forum. The various practices retreated back to their respective contexts, which weakened their ability to reach broader audiences.

Despite the vagueness associated with it, the concept of cyberfeminism has continued to play (or is yet *again* playing) an important role in the search for new technofeminist approaches – be it as an object of nostalgic romanticizing, as an object of critique directed toward its inconsistent political strategies, or as a historical reference to what was then a new era of combining technology and gender. Accordingly, the new wave of interest in cyberfeminism, which began around 2014, is heterogeneous as well. Alongside uncritical and nostalgic attempts to revive cyberfeminism without taking into account the techno-material and techno-political conditions that have since changed,[7] events such as the "Post-Cyberfeminist International" or the "1st <Interrupted = 'Cyfem and Queer'>" festival have aimed

---

5   See Wajcman, *TechnoFeminism*, 63; and Helen Hester's discussion of "political disidentification" in her essay "After the Future: *n* Hypotheses of Post-Cyber Feminism," *Res* (June 30, 2017), http://beingres.org/2017/06/30/afterthefuture-helenhester/ (accessed August 23, 2018).

6   See Cornelia Sollfrank, "Revisiting the Future: Cyberfeminism in the 21st Century," in *Across & Beyond: A Transmediale Reader on Post-Digital Practices, Concepts, and Institutions*, ed. Ryan Bishop et al. (Berlin: Sternberg Press, 2016), 228-47.

7   See, for instance, Sonja Peteranderl, "Die Pionierinnen des Cyberfeminismus sagen den Tech-Cowboys den Kampf an," *WIRED Germany* (June 2, 2015), https://www.wired.de/collection/life/das-cyberfeminismus-kollektiv-vns-matrix-macht-eine-kampfansage; and Claire L. Evans, "We Are the Future Cunt: Cyberfeminism in the 90s," *Motherboard* (November 20, 2014), https://motherboard.vice.com/en_us/article/4x37gb/we-are-the-future-cunt-cyberfeminism-in-the-90s (both articles accessed August 23, 2018).

to combine historical approaches with current practices and to formulate new theoretical positions on the basis of praxis. Meanwhile, an entirely independent concept of cyberfeminism has been developed in Latin America, for instance, where cyberfeminist activists have explicitly defined themselves against their theoretical precursors and have based their understanding of the term exclusively on their own practices.[8] Moreover, xenofeminism, which claims to designate a consistent political approach, can likewise be regarded as an effort to demarcate a clear position within (or perhaps away from) pluralistic cyberfeminism.[9]

The new interest in cyberfeminism is a good starting point for promoting urgently needed contextualizing engagement, for comparing the historical positions of the 1990s with their current iterations, and not least for examining the potential of the concept for approaches that have yet to be developed. What can the concept of cyberfeminism still accomplish today? Can it be adjusted to today's changed conditions, or would it be more sensible to abandon it in favor of new concepts? In any case, it is necessary when using the term to provide some indication of how it is being understood.

At any rate, the great techno-political transformations of recent decades require us to remove our cyber-glasses for a moment and look at the patch of earth where we are standing, and even though our gaze is directed toward the future, it is necessary for us to look around and see what is happening in our immediate vicinity, with other bodies, other beings, and the inorganic and organic environment. Discourses such as new materialism and queer deconstruction are working to "queer" powerful dichotomies and, by including new agents, to change our understanding of the mechanisms that shape reality. At issue is the "agency of things," that is, the influential effects of material that, though existing outside of language and independent of human volition and behavior, encompasses human beings as material reality – and not the other way around. Queer deconstruction advances the feminist deconstruction of power relations by exposing the mechanisms of "othering" and by expanding into new areas of inquiry: gender, sex, disability, nature, non-human species, machines, the socially and globally vulnerable, and other subalterns. How is *the*

---

8   See the contribution by Spideralex in this volume.

9   See the contribution by Isabel de Sena in this volume.

other, that "is the ideological and cultural foundation for exploitation and oppression," constructed?[10] "Whoever helps to shatter these dualistic hierarchies and move toward complex relations and interrelations among actors is already – one could say – acting in a queer/feminist or ecofeminist manner,"[11] writes Yvonne Volkart, who proposes the term *techno-eco-feminism* to convey her new theory about the interplay of ecological and technofeminist aspects. This new philosophical movement involves thinking about technology not only in conjunction with (socio-)political and cultural, but also with material and ecological categories.

Although certain figures of thought associated the term techno-eco-feminism with new materialism, and the methods of queer deconstruction may be new, their underlying idea of creating a connection between various ecologies – environment/ecology, the social ecology, and the mental ecology – was already present in Félix Guattari's writings from the 1980s.[12] Among other things, Guattari's "ecosophy" is an appeal to expand our notion of what ecologies contain and, by conceptually integrating previously separate spheres, to place something in opposition to the prevailing active and passive destruction of the environment and the "reductive approach of scientism." Genuine transformation is not possible without understanding the inherent connections between these different spheres and without acknowledging that the construction of their separation is an instrument of power. Guattari attributed a central role to the then widely imagined potential of nascent interactive media – that is, what we would call the internet today – for he believed that they would liberate individuals from their passivity and enable new forms of collective action. The precise extent to which these new media are themselves embedded in the ideological, power-political, and material conditions that created and configured them would only come to light with their global dissemination. And it is precisely these factors that the technofeminism of the early twenty-first century had set out

---

10 Quoted from Yvonne Volkart's article in this volume.

11 Ibid.

12 See Félix Guattari, *The Three Ecologies,* trans. Ian Pindar and Paul Sutton (London: Athlone Press, 2000 [originally published in 1989]); and idem, "Remaking Social Practices," trans. Sophie Thomas, in *The Guattari Reader,* ed. Gary Genosko (Oxford: Blackwell, 1996), 262-72.

to examine. Just as nothing can exist outside of technology, technology itself is always permeated by the conditions of its origination.

As mentioned above, another important precursor to today's technofeminist positions is Donna Haraway, who not only paved the way with her early works but has also, with what she abbreviates as "SF" (which can stand for both "science fiction" and "speculative feminism"), spent the last thirty years gaining intriguing and inspiring perspectives from apparently hopeless, man-made catastrophe scenarios. In her most recent books, she focuses on what she calls the "Chthulucene" to develop the idea of an age of "sympoiesis" – an era characterized by the togetherness and cooperation of multiple species (humans included) – and thus she has not only contributed to the decentering of the subject, but has also supplemented certain new-materialist approaches to understanding the material world of both human and non-human "nature."[13] Out of cyberfeminism, which has been concerned above all with the opportunities of deterritorialization and immaterialization, certain overarching, interlocking, and transversal positions have developed that are no longer content to operate simply with symbols and information in virtual space but are rather interested in integrating diverse spaces and qualities in an effort to improve life itself.

Their differences aside, what all of these new transgressive, intersectional, and integrative movements have in common is an attitude of *care* or *concern*. In many ways, they are caring, worrying, ready to take responsibility, anchored in the here and now, and on the lookout for new types of relations. While searching for answers to global and local problems, engaging in scientific research, and devising technological solutions, this attitude of care contributes to the establishment of a new form of knowledge, a knowledge that rejects objectivization and is interested not only in observations and representations but also in transformations – in forging relations with things, in being affected, and thus in changing itself and the world in a process of co-transformation.[14] Joan C. Tronto and Berenice Fischer have defined caring

---

13 See Donna Haraway, *The Companion Species Manifesto: Dogs, People, and Significant Otherness* (Chicago: Prickly Paradigm Press, 2015); and eadem, *Staying with the Trouble: Making Kin in the Chthulucene* (Durham, NC: Duke University Press, 2016).

14 See Maria Puig de la Bellacasa, "Ein Gefüge vernachlässigter Dinge'," in: *Ökologien der Sorge*, ed. Tobias Bärtsch et al. (Vienna: transversal texts, 2017, 137-88).

as "everything that we do to maintain, continue, and repair "our" world so that we can live in it as well as possible. That world includes our bodies, our selves, and our environment, all of which we seek to interweave in a complex, life-sustaining web."[15] In light of technofeminist praxis, caring requires us to understand technological webs not only as objects but also as nodes of social and political interest. It also means that we have to intervene in the production of knowledge, science, and technology.

Here, care abandons its traditional territory of reproduction and begins to enter into a relationship with the complexities of technology and technoscience – and particularly their destructive aspects. The aim is to responsibly include everyone and everything involved in the becoming of things, to expand anthropocentric politics, and thus to do justice to the material meaning of caring. For this, it is necessary to invent new connections between humans and machines, namely connections based on relationships of care and concern.

In his essay "Remaking Social Practices," Guattari acknowledges that it can be difficult "to bring individuals out of themselves, to disengage themselves from their immediate preoccupations, in order to reflect on the present and the future of the world,"[16] and he remarks that the collective impulses to do so are lacking. The positions presented in this book are meant to provide these impulses. Each is complex in itself and linked to its own network of references, discourses, persons, and other agents. They are indicative of a diversity of (often marginalized) experiences that are reflected not least in their heterogeneous formats and writing styles. Here, by way of summary, I can only relate a few of their highlights.

Technofeminist Positions

Sophie Toupin describes feminist hacking as a dual expansion, though one might also call it a "double hack." On the one hand, it adds a material dimension to traditional technofeminism, and on the other hand it expands the concept of "hacking," which typically refers to

---

15 This definition, which Tronto and Fischer formulated together, is quoted here from Tronto's book *Moral Boundaries: A Political Argument for an Ethic of Care* (New York: Routledge, 1993), 103.

16 Guattari, "Remaking Social Practices," 263.

technical categories such as software and hardware, to include "gender" as an area of application. This movement is made possible by understanding gender as technology. Gender is not thought of as something (biologically) given, but rather as something that is always being renewed by the heterogeneous cultural processes that make it mutable. Proceeding from formational cultural techniques makes it possible to steer conditions toward the production of the conditions in question, that is, toward the processes that lead to their production. The basis for this is an understanding of sex as technology, an understanding that Teresa de Lauretis (inspired by Foucault) transferred to a "technology of gender" in the mid-1980s and thus contributed in an essential manner to freeing gender from the binary conception of sexual difference, replacing difference with heterogeneity, and replacing naturally given bodies with complex political strategies for naturalization.[17] "An understanding of gender and the human body as technology," according to Toupin, "makes the praxis of hacking much more accessible because, for feminists, this is a more familiar point of entry." What is essential is that feminist hacking entails a combination of technical competence, feminist principles, and socio-political engagement. Here, unlike the case in traditional hacker environments, technical competence is not something pursued for its own sake – or for the sake of recognition within the meritocratic hierarchies of hacker culture – but is rather a necessary precondition for promoting emancipatory aspects when developing or dealing with technology. Prominent feminist principles of the new hacker culture include collectivity in the form of common action, informal and formal transfers of knowledge on the basis of feminist pedagogy, and the production of visibility – and not in the sense of individual or collective positions, but rather in the sense of exposing hidden mechanisms of the technological realm, of the "off-spaces" that are never in the picture and yet are constitutive for what is seen. Such things include the physical, economic, and material structures in which technologies are embedded. The foundation of this emancipatory and oppositional culture is a redefinition of the relation between online and offline spaces, which is in turn based on the production of its own new spaces and structures.

---

17 See Andrea Seier, *Remediatisierung: Die performative Konstruktion von Gender und Medien* (Berlin: LIT, 2007), 26-32.

Spideralex has put together a collective document for this publication. Through her activity for the Gender and Technology Institute, which trains physical and psycho-social security, for a variety of activists, artivists, lawyers, journalists, and privacy advocates, she has had the opportunity to collaborate with a number of diverse groups and initiatives. For her text, she has chosen 24 positions that are representative of Latin-American cyberfeminism. The ideas of the groups/persons/initiatives come to expression in the form of quotations, to which Spideralex has added comments of her own. The living conditions to which the activists refer in their remarks and their descriptions of quotidian violence are shocking testaments to multiple forms of oppression: They live in postcolonial countries and have limited access to education and careers; they live in political systems lacking freedom of speech and thus under the influence of sinister alliances between the drug mafia, the church, government corruption, and machismo – alliances that are especially predisposed to repress women and gender activists. Although attacks have been increasing in the global North as well – both in their frequency and intensity[18] – the manifold possibilities of digital communication seem to have strengthened Latin America's macho culture in a particular way. Thus it is no surprise that the most important point of Spideralex's collection is concerned with (cyber-)feminist self-defense. Above all, this means protection from violence, both online and offline. To this end, the strategies of these cyberfeminists include emotional, physical (martial arts), and technical support;[19] the provision of safer spaces for raising awareness and for common learning; and collective self-care. The terms that recur frequently throughout the texts are "solidarity," "sorority" (sisterly love), "commonality," and "collectivity," concepts that sound almost pathetic from a "comfortable distance," that is, in hyper-individualized, alienated, neoliberal, and post-capitalist industrial societies where such words are flung around as empty formulas and at best seem to appear in marketing campaigns for consumer products. Here, however, in light of the real threat to physical and mental integrity, they are once again filled with meaning. Thus this is not simply a matter of permanent struggle but of war – a war that

---

18 See Christina Grammatikopoulou's contribution in this volume.

19 See   https://gendersec.tacticaltech.org/wiki/index.php/Complete_manual   (accessed August 24, 2018).

Latin-American cyberfeminists are willing to engage in on all levels. Their understanding of cyberfeminism does not, as they repeatedly stress, derive from their artistic and academic predecessors from the global North, but is rather based on their praxis alone, a praxis that has arisen first and foremost from their threatening circumstances. That said, many of their practices and the concepts associated with them exhibit a striking similarity to current academic discourses about the expanded notions of ecology and care, as in the combination of ecofeminism and technofeminism or in the economies of open access, free software, and open content. Technology is no longer thought of as a separate sphere but rather as being embedded in material and ideological means of production. More than just a reaction to circumstances, their fight will not come to an end until, with furious determination, they actualize a vision of the future full of happiness and devoid of fear. The path in that direction is not straight, however, but will involve not only reflecting on but also transforming the material conditions in which they and their actions are embedded.

A specific instrument for raising awareness of a given community's culture of communication – of its marginalizing or discriminatory nature, for instance – is the so-called "code of conduct." In her contribution to this book, Femke Snelting reflects on her own experiences in creating such a regulatory framework in the community of Libre Graphics Meetings, and she examines the origins, orientation, and specific features of this code in the case of certain free-software projects. Among other important things, such documents are intended to promote inclusion and diversity, prevent assault and harassment as much as possible, implement conflict-resolution strategies to prevent escalation, and, in specific cases of misconduct, introduce punitive measures. When codes of conduct are treated as living documents and not simply as a way to transfer responsibility away from individuals, they can in fact counteract inappropriate and harassing behavior within the framework of a binding community, as is evident from a number of feminist hacker initiatives. The author identifies their feminist potential in the fact that working to produce such a document creates a platform for self-reflection where everyone involved learns to question his or her own behavior, to discuss and formulate common values, and to translate these values into everyday practices. This does not mean that a community will automatically become safer or more diverse – despite the existence of such codes of conduct in the world of free software, 97% of the developers are still white and male – but environments that have worked out a code of conduct have proved to be more acutely aware of (and actively opposed to) discriminatory and repressive behavior. A code of conduct can thus be seen as a sort of invitation for diversity. The area of free software is closely attuned to the power and influence of language; codes and programs, after all, are nothing but behavioral instructions, and the step of reflecting and drafting a code for one's own behavior can of course be taken in many other areas of life as well. Especially in the case of temporary events and short-term projects, there is much need for self-reflection and for the establishment of consistent codes of conduct in order to foster safe and inviting conditions. The potential of these types of guidelines is thus far from exhausted.

In the wake of the first German publication of the "Feminist Principles of the Internet," the activist hvale vale tells her story of working on the project and provides insight into how the document was created. The Association for Progressive Communications (APC) undertook the initiative in 2014, when it invited more than fifty activists (mainly from the global South) to Malaysia. After several meetings and a multi-year discussion process involving more than one hundred women and representatives of the queer community, seventeen principles were formulated by combining elements from the feminist human-rights movement and the internet-justice movement. The foundations of these efforts were intersectionality and the assumptions that technology and the internet are not neutral and that the internet is not a tool but rather a space in which resistance is just as necessary as it is elsewhere. The co-created document is understood to be a work in progress – as a platform and a community – and anyone interested is invited to participate in the translation and distribution of the principles (or simply to "live by them"). In addition to demanding access and economic solidarity, they also focus on promoting informational and sexual self-determination: "They [the principles] are inscribed in the digital age. They come in and out of the internet and in and out of our bodies. They stand for feelings and pleasure, but also for justice and rights." Like every collective gesture that claims to be universally valid and yet is based on locality, embodiment, and diversity, the "Feminist Principles of the Internet" and their internal contradictions offer a productive basis for further work and further thinking.

In her text, Christina Grammatikopoulou investigates a series of contemporary art and protest phenomena, which she refers to as viral performances of gender, and she classifies these performances according to the strategies that each has employed. The projects chosen for her analysis take place either exclusively online, where they test out social media as new milieus for performative interventions, or they operate in a combination of online and offline space in order to experiment with the mutually conditioned dynamics of viral dissemination. The online performances address such themes as body positivity, sexual assault, and gender stereotyping by blurring the lines between true and false, between consent and manipulation. From her many examples, Grammatikopoulou extracts two fundamental concepts, which she refers to as "noise" and "virality." Noise she defines as "a manipulative communication strategy [...] which, through the conscious disruption or muddling of communication platforms, aims to obfuscate or falsify information or a message for its receiver or to spread false information." The goal of the second strategy, virality, is to have content spread horizontally and as widely as possible by users themselves. For this to succeed, the content in question needs to have a certain "quality" (it may, for instance, be humorous, provocative, or simply catchy), but it also requires a feedback loop between bodies on the street and online images, which in turn attract more people onto the street. Grammatikopoulou positions all the various phenomena of contemporary feminism that she has investigated along a spatial continuum spanning from online to offline, a continuum which she refers to as "expanded space." Her insightful classification of today's feminisms is not, however, concerned with providing precise definitions of content, and thus the question of where and how transformations have taken place is often left unanswered. Her goal is rather to bring to light irresolvable contradictions – ambiguities between activism and noise, between empowerment and self-objectification, between consumer culture and political concerns – in order, in the end, to claim that contemporary feminism has come to be defined by precisely that: the blurring of formerly clear boundaries and relations. Thus it is no surprise that many of the concepts and strategies that she has identified are also being employed in other political circles by anti-feminists of all sorts, a fact that raises, yet again, the old feminist question concerning the interplay between structure and content ...

In her contribution, Yvonne Volkart opens up a new dimension in the technofeminist debate. As indicated by the title of her article – "Techno-Eco-Feminism" – she attempts to integrate two antagonistic feminist approaches, ecofeminism and technofeminism, in order to create a transversal space for thinking and acting that is based on relationality and is suited to the complex situation of the Anthropocene. Proceeding from the threatening scenario of humankind's potential extinction, Volkart describes how the concerns of early ecofeminism have been reformulated by current techno-ecological trends and how these new concerns have inpired some of the most innovative approaches to leading a participatory life in today's "naturecultures."[20] Although the ecofeminism of the 1970s anticipated the central postulates of the debate about today's ecological crises, its parallel treatment of the oppression of women in the patriarchy and the exploitation of nature (and the environmental destruction associated with it) often led to essentialist statements about the social relations between nature and gender. Especially as it was practiced in the United States, ecofeminism presupposed a positive relationship between women and nature (often with reference to women's reproductive abilities), and thus blamed men and their use of technology for the suppression and exploitation of nature. The movement thus catered to controversy, beckoned to be rejected, and fostered a generally critical and dismissive attitude toward technology. Distancing themselves from this position, European ecofeminists emphasized early on a social-constructivist understanding of gender and refrained from representing women as caring and men as destructive and exploitative. More recent queer ecologies have taken this anti-essentialism further by deconstructing the "naturalness" of biological reproduction processes and the production of life. At the heart of this critique is not only the naturalization of

---

20 Coined by Donna Haraway, the term "natureculture" denotes the co-origination of nature and culture. According to Christine Bauhardt, it represents an interesting attempt "to dissolve the binary opposition of both constructs and give linguistic expression to their essential inner connection." See Christine Bauhardt, "Feministische Ökonomie, Ökofeminismus und Queer Ecologies – Feministisch-materialistische Perspektiven auf gesellschaftliche Naturverhältnisse," *Gender Politik Online* (April 2012), https://www.fuberlin.de/sites/gpo/pol_theorie/Zeitgenoessische_ansaetze/Bauhardtfemoekonomie/Bauhardt.pdf (accessed August 26, 2018).

gender and heterosexuality, but also a concern about developing specifically situated, "polychromatic" approaches to multispecies. Every reference to natural "givens" is cast into question. For such thinkers, "nature" is always preformed by the construction of a heteronormative gender binary, and it functions as a generalizing, compensatory, and romanticizing antithesis to the use of technology in capitalism. As Bauhardt has summarized: "The queer perspective dissolves the unfortunate amalgamation of sexuality, nature, and gender in order to negotiate the social conditions of reproduction on a new basis."[21] Eco-techno-feminism rounds out this discourse by including technology – and techniques. As forms of biopower, capitalist technologies themselves produce life. For this reason, they can no longer be regarded, as they were in the 1970s, as instruments of liberation or oppression distinct from bodies, material, and the environment. Unsullied nature does not exist, and there is nothing that can be called "the nature" or "the technology." Rather, there are only specific movements, sedimentations, and interrelations in the manifold constellations of technocultures, capital, and material entities. Thus it is essential to expand our perspective to include the interactions of diverse sets of agents. Materiality, which has hitherto been neglected, has come back and been identified as having its own agency and influence.[22] This act of further decentering the subject involves understanding material as living, artefactual, and relational.

Volkart develops her theory of queer-feminist, techno-ecological relationality on the basis of contemporary works of art. In doing so, she illustrates that the ways of thinking and acting associated with these works derive from a feminist tradition, but that now, to the extent that they pose "questions about coexistence, about plant and animal rights, empathy and care, healing and repairing," they have begun "to enter into dominant theoretical and artistic discourses." Not least, this has also begun to affect everyday practices and activism. Thinking about social and ecological crises together – a long neglected process – is reflected in the desire for vitality, presence, affect, and relationality from which transformational power can emerge in the face of catastrophic scenarios.

---

21 Ibid.

22 See Karen Barad's concept of "agential realism."

In the final chapter, Isabel de Sena initiates a long-overdue critique of xenofeminism by taking a closer look at some of its fundamental concepts. The concept of xenofeminism, which is directly associated with the Laboria Cuboniks collective and its manifesto, is a difficult one to penetrate because of the affective language and the high level of abstraction with which the group develops its theses. Active since 2014, and alternating between an artistic prank and a genuine political movement, the group has performed at numerous events in the art scene without yet invoking any serious objections to the content of its work, which, as de Sena demonstrates, in part is not just extremely provocative, but also contrary to some of the basic principles of feminism. Here the author does what no one has done before: She takes the concepts and theses of the manifesto seriously and gets to the bottom of some of them. Although her piece is meant and formulated as just a preliminary commentary – and not as a fundamental critique – it quickly becomes clear that the many inconsistencies and contradictions festering beneath the shiny, futuristic surfaces of their arguments frustrate the xenofeminist demand for logic and reason. And not only that: Despite its many original and discussion-worthy ideas, it seems as though it would be difficult, if not impossible, to translate xenofeminism into a praxis of any sort. The critique formulated here hopes to instigate a dialog for the sake of transposing xenofeminism and thus making it connectable to other (techno-)feminisms of the 21st century.

FEMINIST HACKING.

Resistance through Spaciality

Sophie Toupin

AYESHA[1] SEES HERSELF AS A FEMINIST HACKER. HER TWITTER HANDLE is @FemHacking. Her influence on the net has been growing steadily for some time now. Unfortunately, a group of people decided that Ayesha was getting too much attention online, and made it their mission to silence and discredit her. An army of *trolls* attacked her for weeks, sending hurtful comments and messages to belittle her on Twitter. She has even received email threats against her physical integrity. In response to this situation, Ayesha first contacted Twitter to report the online violence she was experiencing, and then blocked some of the people who were harassing her. She also used the "Block Together" function to share blocked troll lists with other users on

---

1   Her name and pseudonym on Twitter have been changed to avoid revealing the identity of the person.

Twitter, as well as the "Block Bot" function to block known stalkers on Twitter. Moreover, her research on how she can react to the negative effects of trolls has led her to use Foxxydoxing, a script that helped her analyse the connections between her attackers on Twitter.

Ayesha is not a neophyte of the web, nor of technology. She studied at the Birla Institute of Technology and Science in Pilani and works as a freelance programmer. She is familiar with the different tools she can use to respond to an attack, as well as to protect her personal data. She is also one of the co-founders of a feminist hackspace, a space where queer and trans women meet to discuss feminist hacking, as well as to organize training workshops such as feminist encryption (femcrypts), cell phone jail breaking, mutual aid computer support, and other thematic workshops of all kinds. Her extensive knowledge and concrete online actions have enabled her to make her self-defence against the trolls more effective. And she also thought about responding directly to trolls, but decided it might be too difficult to engage in this struggle on her own.

During a meeting in the feminist hackspace she co-founded, Ayesha shared her experience of online harassment with the aim of finding other ways to solve the problem with the help of others. One of her colleagues advised her to subscribe to the Gender and Tech Institute (GTI) mailing list, which recently had announced the feminist project ZeroTrollerance, which aims to "re-educate" trolls. In addition, the members of this list had initiated a solidarity action online by creating feminist bots, i.e. computer scripts that allow automated messages to be sent and trolls to be attacked collectively. The idea behind this action was also to generate public debate, thus drawing attention to this type of harassment.

The above example is not an isolated case. Many active feminists who raise their voice on the Internet have become victims of online harassment. In response to this violence, feminists from different backgrounds are organizing collectively to address these situations. Thanks to their actions, these experienced technofeminists are creating new feminist resistance practices in the field of technology. Their collective thinking, years of activism and technical skills also lead to the creation of autonomous feminist infrastructures such as servers, discussion lists and bots. When they speak of "infrastructures," they refer to software and hardware, but also spaces such as hackspaces as well as social and technical solidarity. By using the term "autonomous," they express their desire to rethink forms of resistance against a system of production and values that they categorize as capitalist, racist and patriarchal (Editor's note, 2015).

Although some self-identify as technofeminists, feminist hacktivists, transhack feminists, makers or feminist geeks, they are increasingly referred to the generic term "feminist hackers," i.e. hackers who engage in feminist hacking practices. The adjective "feminist" makes the difference to the conventional "hacker" by indicating a specific form of politicized practice.

My interpretation of feminist hacking practice, as I present it below, is based on my own experience as a participant and/or co-organizer of the spaces, as well as an activist teacher and researcher in some of the groups mentioned here. Thereafter, I turn my attention to feminist hackspaces that are an integral part of the new feminist hacking culture. Finally, this article aims to reveal some of the specificities of feminist hacking by proposing key principles of their resistance practices and spatial effects, including the practice of working together, the politics of visibility, the co-production of knowledge, solidarity and awareness of the materiality of technology.

I would like to point out that many of the ideas in this article are not the result of my unique observations, but rather of a co-production of knowledge through many virtual and physical encounters in which I have participated, and which have been spread over many years. These ideas are the product of a collective reflection on what feminist hacking means and what feminist hackspaces are. Whether the meeting spaces are physical or virtual does not play an essential role; what matters, in my opinion, is that the method of "doing it together" is emphasized; all those who, through their years of collaboration, dialogue, and countless contributions, have contributed to the common production of knowledge, discourse, and practice, should be recognized. Acknowledging co-production as part of the history is part of a feminist approach that credits women, queers and transgendered people for contributing their specific knowledge (Mohanty, 2003; Sandoval, 2000). However, I remain the sole author of this article and my interpretation as well as the emphasis on certain aspects of this practice of resistance, are shaped by my own attitude and subjectivity. In doing so, I anchor this article in a more classical literature review, as well as on documents created by feminist hackers. By making visible the co-construction of knowledge, I wish to highlight the symbiosis between practice and theory, in addition to recognizing that the reflections and discussions that are at the very root of feminist hacking practices are above all collective and always in motion.

Feminist Hackspaces

Gabriella Coleman describes the hacker and hacking much more broadly. She defines it as "a technologist with a penchant for computing" and hacking as "a clever technical solution arrived at through non-obvious means" (Coleman, 2014: 1). Feminist hackers draw inspiration from this broad definition as a starting point, but extend the concept by moving it away from technology and computer science (Nguyen, Toupin and Barzell 2016; Toupin, 2013, 2014;). Their idea is, first of all, to hack the concept of hacking itself and thus attract the attention of all feminists who have little to do with hacking in the technical sense. By understanding gender or the human body as technologies as well, as entities that can be hacked, i.e. transformed, they are able to reach out to a group that would otherwise not be affected by the traditional notion of hacking.

Considering gender or the human body as a technology (Sofia, 2000) makes hacking much more accessible by creating familiar entry points for feminists. Since gender can be culturally shaped and reshaped by feminist hackers, digital technology can also be recoded in a feminist way. According to this conception, the values embedded in digital technologies as well as in gender can be reprogrammed. The anchoring of this practice in everyday life and the use of a familiar gender concept help to bring this practice within the reach of feminists and arouse their interest. Thus, the idea of feminist hacking has inspired many people to include body hacking or gender hacking. Forlano (2016), for example, identifies with the practice of body hacking and even compares herself to a cyborg to articulate how she takes care of her diabetic body. She is developing a feminist analysis of hacking through an auto-ethnographic account of her early years as a type 1 diabetic that forces her to use an insulin pump and a glucose monitor. She describes herself as a cyborg to emphasize her new hybridity, that is, her skin, bones and blood must constantly harmonize with sensors, tubes and other external devices to keep her alive.

In recent years, the craze for body hacking, a practice that can sometimes be quite individual, has quietly given way to collective responses to online violence, since the latter is omnipresent and requires an urgent response. Indeed, this type of intervention is emerging as one of the leading practices of feminist hacking through the creation of feminist collective spaces, both virtual and physical. It is important to note that there are several feminist hacking currents influenced by different social, economic, political, geographical and historical contexts. This practice is also constantly in motion, constituting and renewing itself temporally.[2]

The emergence of a new feminist hacking culture becomes visible through various resistance practices and is organized, among other things, through meetings at various fixed, changing, or spontaneously determined locations. In the United States, most feminist hackspaces adopt an intersectional feminist perspective that emphasizes the interaction between gender and other identity variables such as race and social class when addressing inequality, oppression and violence (Toupin, 2013, 2014; Crenshaw, 1991; Moraga and Anzaldúa, 1983). Some are only open to women, queers and trans people, while others are open to all those who identify themselves as feminists. The question of who is allowed to self-identify as feminist, and therefore can become involved in feminist hackspaces, is therefore not uniform. Rather, it is the group constituting each feminist hackspace that defines its own policy of access and participation. At the root of feminist hackspaces is the desire to co-create so-called "safe" spaces where well-being (care) is central (Goldenberg, 2014; Toupin, 2014). This practice of well-being (Goldenberg, 2014) differs from more traditional hackspaces that adopt an open space policy. The work of researcher Alison Adam (2003), on which Goldenberg (2014) is based, highlights the ethics of caring for women hackers that complicates hacker ethics as described by Steven Levy (2010).[3] For Adam and

---

2   Because of this fluidity, it is difficult to define exactly what feminist hacking is. FemHack, a Montréal-based collective of feminist hackers, seeks to lay the foundation for feminist hacking by emphasizing the desire for autonomy, freedom, self-organization, and mutual help that feminist hackers share in their relationship to Internet technologies and knowledge.

3   Hacker ethics includes the importance of sharing, decentralization, openness and access to computers. In addition, this ethic argues that hackers should be judged for their hacking skills, not on criteria such as gender, age, race, or socio-economic position.

Goldenberg, it is essential to take into consideration gender, ethnicity and, more generally, the social privileges associated with different identities, as these have an influence on the future hacker. In addition, feminist hackers are also called upon to take care of each other emotionally and physically to deal with harassment. As a complement to their understanding of the ethics of care and well-being, feminist hackers point out that the debate on questions of privilege and meritocracy within the so-called traditional hackspaces is too weak. Why are there very few people of colour or women in these so-called "open" spaces? Do these spaces reinforce a dominant informal culture? These questions are essential for feminist hackers, since they are intrinsically linked to their ethics on the one hand, and to a desire for awareness within the hacker culture on the other hand (Toupin, 2013). To demonstrate their point, feminist hackers cite Jo Freeman's (1972) article entitled "The Tyranny of Structurelessness," which warns against the idealization of open spaces. In her work, Freeman argues that the absence of formal structures in a group or space ultimately favours those who already have privileges (gender, class, sexual orientation, race, etc.) and facilitates the informal power of certain individuals or cliques. Rather than opting for an open space policy, feminist hackspaces therefore establish very concrete guidelines for creating safe and emancipatory spaces of well-being, such as delimiting who can take part in feminist hackspaces' activities.

The fact that more and more temporary and/or mobile feminist spaces are emerging is due to a certain economic situation[4] and can at best be understood as a complementary strategy for the creation of permanent spaces. These temporary feminist spaces have emerged, for example, within the very heart of the world's largest hacker conferences such as the Chaos Communication Congress (CCC) or the Chaos Communication Camp (CCC). They have also emerged from feminist tech meetings such as /ETC (Eclectic Tech Carnival) and the TransHackFeminist (THF!) convergences. All these gatherings in an ad hoc common place have made it possible to co-construct the practice of feminist hacking in a transnational way. This practice thus goes beyond the local or national level and allows identification with

---

4   Many feminist hacking collectives simply do not have the financial means to pay
    a monthly rent, which is why they opt for the mobile variant. Meetings can there-
    fore take place in a café, in an activist room or at one of their members' premises.

transnational resistance practices and solidarity. At these meetings, the affirmation of a collective self is articulated and new feminist hacking approaches can emerge. Thus a sense of belonging to this new culture is developed, which is in the process of being created and, for the time being, is a marginal phenomenon. Feminist hacking thus provides a framework for analysis, a common vocabulary, and the encounters of feminist hackers strengthen their ties and their desire for a mutual project. These gatherings also emphasize the importance of a feminist hacking approach and make it possible, for example, to exchange possible strategies in the fight against (online) sexism and violence, to jointly produce knowledge and to experiment with different forms of feminist pedagogy. Projects such as feminist servers, which will be discussed below, also emerged from these common meetings and desires for autonomous feminist infrastructure.

Transformative practices

In this section, I look at the specificities of feminist hacking practice, highlighting some of its spatial effects. More specifically, I am interested in the following aspects: doing it together, the politics of visibility, the co-production of knowledge and solidarity, and the materiality of technology.

The practice of "Doing it Together"

The practice of "Doing it Together" is at the root of the feminist hacking approach, which has developed mainly as a learning pedagogy to enable novices, in particular, to gain confidence in their technical skills, while reinforcing the idea of solidarity and co-production of knowledge. This learning pedagogy is not in opposition to Do It Yourself (DIY), but rather complements it.

Doing things together is also a practice of resistance, because, instead of the heroic deeds of an expert, collectivity is emphasized. Of course, the predominant stories of hacker culture are fascinating, but they often revolve only around legendary figures and their computer exploits (Lapsley, 2013; Levy, 2010). As a result, other forms of dealing with technology do not receive enough recognition (Dunbar-Hester, 2016). In addition, the male representation of computer hacking in the press and popular culture creates a form of exclusion. By creating new imaginary worlds that unfold across all physical and virtual spaces, with an emphasis on community, feminist hackers attempt to deconstruct and change old role models.

The policy of visibility

The practices of feminist hackers are part of a strategy to create visibility that increasingly pushes itself into public perception through the affirmation of a collective self–both in physical places and on the net. The politics of visibility also serve at "bringing to light the invisible infra/structures of power that render technological achievement possible" (Nguyen, Toupin and Bardzell, 2016:1). By promoting a different way of using technology, that is feminist and in resistance to patriarchy and capitalist exploitation, feminist hackers propose a real alternative to the status quo and thus practice a unique approach. For feminist hackers, technology is first and foremost political and by no means neutral (Winner, 1980). They also contradict the position that suggests that violence on the net is due to a few "bad apples" rather than acknowledging that it is part of systemic patriarchal practice. Moreover, feminist hackers no longer consider the Internet as a safe space, and argue that the struggle must take place not only at the discursive level, but also at the material level. Therefore, they try to shed light on what really are digital infrastructures: from the exploitation of minerals in conflict zones to unacceptable working conditions in production facilities to waste management in the technology sector (for example, disposal or incineration of equipment in China or Ghana). Recognising the materiality of technology is integral to understanding the life cycle of technologies. Emphasizing this materiality underscores the impact of technology on the environment, social and neo-colonial relations between the countries of the southern and northern hemispheres.

This feminist resistance was born in direct reaction to the fact that the Internet has become a centralized space for consumption, surveillance and control of dissenting voices by governments, private companies and anti-feminists. Although they recognize the importance of a "counter-public" (Fraser, 1990), especially at the discursive level, they do, however, attach increasing importance to the issue of materiality (Parks and Starosielski, 2015). Counter-publics such as feminist hackspaces or feminist discussion lists are spaces for the production of oppositional ways of understanding identities and interests that are marginalized, not to say excluded, in public space. Since these counter-publics gain a certain visibility on the Internet, those who contribute to their dissemination are often exposed to anti-feminist attacks. The visibility policy of feminist hackers is as much about discourse as it is about the materiality of technologies. Speaking of the materiality of the Panama Canal, Ashley Carse (2012) uses the concept of (in)visibility to demonstrate that technology is political. He argues that "visibility is situated, reflecting an actor's geographical location, cultural assumptions, and nature of his or her labor..." (2012: 543) Based on Carse, Brian Larkin (2013) specifies:

"all visibility is situated and what is background for one person is a daily object of concern for another. The point is not to assert one or another status as an inherent condition of infrastructures but to examine how (in)visibility is mobilized and why." (2013: 336)

Feminist servers are a good example of how feminist hackers create visibility while at the same time pointing to their roots in discourse as well as in the materiality of technology. The following paragraph defines their main principles.

A feminist server:

- Is a situated technology. She[5] [the feminist server] has a sense of context and sees herself as part of an ecology of practice;
- Is run for and by a community that cares enough for her to exist.
- Is built on the materiality of software, hardware and the bodies gathered around her.
- Opens herself to expose processes, tools, sources, habits, patterns.
- Does not strive for continuity. All too often, the talk of transparency is a sign that something is being obscured (division of labor issue).
- Avoids efficiency, user-friendliness, scalability and immediacy, as these could be traps.

---

5   The gender-neutral article for a computer server in English language has been subjected to a sex change in languages that distinguish between male, female and neutral articles; the use of the female pronoun here causes a similar irritation, which should additionally stimulate one to think about gender and technology.

- Knows that networking is actually an awkward, promiscuous and parasitic practice.
- Is autonomous in the sense that she decides for her own dependencies.
- Questions the conditions of service.
- Treats technology as part of a social reality.
- Wants networks to be mutable and read-write accessible.
- Does not confuse security with safety.
- Takes the risk of exposing her insecurity while trying hard not to apologise when she sometimes is not available.
  (Snelting, 2014)[6]

These principles reveal a rooting in the concept of situated knowledges (Haraway, 1988) which emphasizes that what "count[s] as rational accounts of the world are struggles over *how* to see" (Haraway, 1988: 375). Haraway suggests a feminist objectivity through this method. By challenging the idea of what objectivity means, it allows us to "see" differently and forces us to be responsible for the visions we embody in our actions and writings.

Two feminist server projects were (re)started during the TransHackFeminist (THF!) 2014 convergence: the "Systerserver" project, initially launched by Genderchangers and Eclectic Tech Carnival (/etc.), and the "Anarchaserver" project, launched by the people involved in the THF! organization.[7] The first server is to offer online website hosting services, while the second focuses on data hosting. The Anarchaserver uses a media wiki for THF! documentation, and an application to host several WordPress sites. The mailing lists and IRC discussion channels of both servers are moderated to coordinate the different tasks that need to be done both conceptually and technically. For example, give root access to some administrators, discuss issues surrounding the location of the physical server (in which data centre will it be located?), agree on a policy for access to virtual and physical servers, ensure that the initiative is well understood in the context of hacker groups, and teach how to manage a server.

---

6 Freely adapted by the author and by the editor.
7 Further feminist servers exist in Latin and South America.

The co-production of knowledge and solidarity
The initiatives of feminist hackers promote collective learning, which aims to create new common resistance practices, but also transnational solidarity. Several examples illustrate the co-production of knowledge and solidarity that emerges from feminist hacking practices.

The Gender and Technology Institute (GTI) was established in late 2014 with the aim of ensuring more online security for queer and trans women and at the same time establishing an international community of feminist hackers.[8] It quickly developed into an international support network and became an important resource for social solidarity by contributing to a better understanding of and enabling collective responses to the various forms of violence. It is on a private discussion list that collective solutions on a wide range of topics are discussed, although online violence predominates in the discussions. A prime example is the discussion in response to the murder of Pakistani techno queer activist Sabeen Mahmud in April 2015, which led to the creation of a worldwide Feminist Hackathon Day (F3mHack). More than thirty activities were organized as part of this World Day, highlighting the great solidarity between feminist hackers from all over the world and the transnational nature of these initiatives.[9]

At the TransHackFeminist (THF!) meeting there was ample opportunity for the joint production of knowledge and solidarity. The convergence gave the opportunity for lengthy discussions on what transhackfeminism is. "The term 'trans' needs to be understood in a plurality of ways. Trans as a noun, a verb, and a prefix. Being in transition, in transformation, being transgendered, being transversal, transdisciplinary etc. ... The term 'hack' refers to the more traditional act of doing, of taking things apart, of understanding things in a deeper way. But it is also seen as an action and as a performance in order to hack patriarchy, capitalism and other systems of oppression, and by making those systems explicit." (Editor's note, 2015)

The original theoretical and later practical anchoring of THF! comes mainly from a Spanish feminist movement that launched a transfeminist uprising (The WhoreDykeBlackTransFeminist Network, 2010) in 2010. Inspired by the Zapatista movement, this insurrection took

---

8   Another GTI was organised in June 2016 in Ecuador.

9   The 2015 version of the website is available here: http://web.archive.org/web/20150524023518/https://f3mhack.org/index.php/en/

the form of a manifesto addressing issues of intersectionality, linking different forms of oppression while calling for transnational solidarity. At first, this uprising was a discursive intervention, but it eventually led to the emergence of the Pechblendas, a transfeminist hacklab,[10] from which the THF! convergence later emerged. It is within this hacklab that the THF! convergence was born. The creation of many feminist hackspaces in the United States as well as the online violence against several Spanish feminists have reinforced the desire to come together, to join forces, and to take stock of the movement and contributions of feminist hackers through the THF!

It must be said that within the THF itself, a multiplicity of voices and visions of feminist hacking has emerged, demonstrating that this type of feminist convergence and hackspace promote plurality in general. However, even the THF! has not been without its share of ideological clashes and other inconsistencies due to the encounter of different "cultures" and ways of doing things among feminists, queers and trans people. To ease these tensions, the principles of solidarity and affinity between feminist hackers were promoted in addition to participation in concrete and partly independent collective projects.

The example of the two feminist servers illustrates this dynamic.

The two examples of the GTI and the THF! are rooted in what Mohanty (2003) describes as a pedagogy of feminist solidarity that emphasizes the complexities, singularities and interconnection between women's communities, so that power, privilege, willingness to act and to dissent are made visible (2003: 243-244). This type of feminist solidarity acknowledges the different historical, socio-economic, cultural and geographical realities so that it becomes possible to communicate in a more complex way about the resistance practices of feminist hackers.

The materiality of the technology

The creation of common spaces and places raises awareness of the materiality of technology, and helps to understand where these technologies come from, with an emphasis on their manufacturing, often based on the exploitation of female, indigenous, southern or

---

10 In the short history of hackspaces, hacklabs have come to be regarded as more politicized and more strongly anchored in the social movements and above all in the occupation movement (Maxigas 2012).

colonized labour force and through the exploitation of natural resources (Nakamura, 2014; Parks/Starosielski, 2015). In other words, feminist hackers want to emphasize the importance of linking the intangible appearance of the digital age with its significant effects on all social spheres, the world of work and the environment. The "digital world" is therefore not distinct or separable from the "real world;" rather, these two worlds are interconnected. By creating an awareness of the materiality of technology, feminist hackers shed light on the new digital spirit of capitalism embedded in the highly controlled and secret infrastructures of algorithmic governmentality, mass surveillance, and the extraction of minerals and rare metals, essential to the very existence of our digital devices.

The materiality of technology makes it clear that the feminist struggle against violence cannot be located only on the Internet. Although violence often manifests itself online and can spread rapidly through the mechanisms of the network, it is also reflected in forms of production based on the exploitation of labour and natural resources. The resistance practices of feminist hackers therefore extend conventional technofeminism through a more holistic approach. Although this approach is becoming more and more widespread, most of the projects are still in their initial stages.

Conclusion

The practices of feminist hackers are a convincing example of resistance rooted in a socio-political redefinition of the relationship between online and offline spaces, thereby generating an emancipatory culture of resistance. By creating physical spaces (such as hackspaces and feminist convergences such as the THF!) and digital spaces (such as invitation-only mailing lists, collective accounts on Twitter, etc.) to address sexism, online violence and all other forms of discrimination, their projects bring about social change. This social change in turn is reflected in the desire to create new spaces where there is room for a variety of new practices and the values they represent.

Feminist hacking is an expression of our time; an era of precariousness, which through the anthropocene, that is, the impact of human beings on their environment, will even be amplified. Paying attention to the materiality of technology and to technological production cycles increases the awareness of our technological footprint and the responsibility we have for the world and its beings. According to this conception, feminist hackers do not necessarily encourage perfect mastery or control of technologies as an end in itself – an attitude they would describe as masculine. Rather, they are concerned with mastering technology in order to stop violence and, beyond that, to create conditions that make it possible to develop new imaginaries for their lives and the lives of their communities.

Bibliography

Adam, Alison (2003) "Hacking into Hacking: Gender and the Hacker Phenomenon," *ACM SIGCAS Computers and Society*, Volume 33, Number 4: 1-15.

Carse, Ashley (2012) "Nature as infrastructure: Making and managing the Panama Canal watershed," *Social Studies of Science*, Volume 42, Number 4: 539-563.

Coleman, Gabriella (2014) "Hackers," *The Johns Hopkins Encyclopedia of Digital Textuality*, http://gabriellacoleman.org/wp-content/uploads/2013/04/Coleman-Hacker-John-Hopkins-2013-Final.pdf.

Crenshaw, Kimberlé (1991) "Mapping the Margins: Intersectionality, Identity Politics and Violence Against Women of Color," *Stanford Law Review*, Volume 43, Number 6: 1241-1299.

Dunbar-Hester, Christina (2016) "Geeks," in Benjamin, P. (Ed.): *Digital Keywords*, Princeton: Princeton University Press: 149-157.

Forlano, Laura (2016) "Hacking the Feminist Disabled Body," *Feminism and (un) hacking, Journal of Peer production,* Volume 8. Available at http://peerproduction.net/issues/issue-8-feminism-and-unhacking/peer-reviewed-papers/hacking-the-feminist-disabled-body/

Fraser, Nancy (1990) "Rethinking the Public Sphere: A Contribution to the Critique of Actually Existing Democracy," *Social Text*, Volume 8, Number 25/26: 56–80.

Freeman, Jo (1972) "The tyranny of structurelessness. The Second Wave." Available at http://struggle.ws/hist_texts/structurelessness.html

Goldenberg, Anne (2014) "Hacking with Care: Attention, bien-être et politique de l'ordinaire dans le milieu hacktiviste," *Magazine DPI*. Available at http://dpi.studioxx.org/fr/hacking-care-attention-bien-%C3%AAtre-et-politique-de-l%E2%80%99ordinaire-dans-le-milieu-hacktiviste

Haraway, Donna (1988) "Situated Knoweldges: The Science Question in Feminism and the Privilege of Partial Perspective," in *Feminist Theory Reader: Local and Global Perspectives*, 2nd ed., eds. McCann, C. and Kim, S. New York, Routledge: 370-383.

Lapsley, Phil (2013) *Exploding the Phone: The Untold Story of the Teenagers and Outlaws Who Hacked Ma Bell*, Grove Press.

Larkin, Brian (2013) "The Politics and Poetics of Infrastructure," *Annual Review of Anthropology*, Volume 42: 327-343.

Levy, Steven (2010) *Hackers: Heroes of the Computer Revolution*, O'Reilly Media.

Maxigas (2012) "Hacklabs and Hackerspaces – Tracing Two Genealogies," *Journal of Peer Production*, Volume 2: 1-10. Available at http://peerproduction.net/issues/issue-2/peer-reviewed-papers/hacklabs-andhackerspaces/

Mohanty, Chandra Talpade (2003) *Feminism without borders: decolonizing theory, practicing solidarity*, Durham: Duke University Press.

Moraga, Cherríe and Anzaldua, Gloria (1983) "This bridge called my back: writings by radical women of color," Kitchen Table, New York: Women of Color Press .

Nakamura, Lisa (2014) "Indigenous Circuits: Navajo Women and the Racialization of Early Electronic Manufacture," *American Quarterly*, Volume 66, Number 4: 919-941.

Nguyen, Lilly, Toupin, Sophie and Bardzell, Shaowen (2016) "Feminist Hacking/Making: Exploring New Gender Horizons of Possibility," Special Issue of the *Journal of Peer Production, Feminism and (un) Hacking*, Volume 8: 1-16.

Parks, Lisa and Starosielski, Nicole (2015): *Signal Traffic: Critical Studies of Media Infrastructures*, Urbana: University of Illinois Press.

Sandoval, Chela (2000) *Methodology of the oppressed*, Minneapolis: University of Minnesota Press.

Snelting, Femke (2014) *A feminist server*. Available at http://esc.mur.at/de/werk/feminist-server

Sofia, Zoe (2000) "Container technologies," *Hypatia*, Volume 15, Number 2: 181-219.

N.D.: "THF! Convergence Report" (2015). Available at https://transhackfeminist.noblogs.org/post/2015/01/25/a-transhackfeminist-thf-convergence-report/

The WhoreDykeBlackTransFeminist Network: *Manifesto for the Trans-Feminist Insurrection* (2010). Available at http://anarchalibrary.blogspot.ca/2010/10/manifesto-for-trans-feminist.html

Toupin, Sophie (2014) "Feminist Hackerspaces: The Synthesis of Feminist and Hacker Cultures," Special Issue on Shared Machines Shops, *Journal of Peer Production*, Volume 5: 1-9.

Toupin, Sophie (2013) "Feminist Hackerspaces as Safer Spaces?," *DPI magazine*. Available at http://dpi.studioxx.org/fr/feminist-hackerspaces-safer-spaces

Winner, Langdon (1980) "Do artifacts have politics?," *Daedelus*, Volume 109, Number 1: 121-136.

This text is an abridged version of "Le hacking féministe: la résistance par la spacialité," Bonenfant, M., F. Dumais and G. Trépanier-Jobin, *Les pratiques transformatrices des espaces socionumériques*, Québec: Presses de l'Université du Québec, 2017. Translation and publication in English with the kind permission of the publisher.

CREATING NEW WORLDS

With Cyberfeminist Ideas and Practices

Text compiled by Spideralex

Translated by Cornelia Sollfrank

Voices (listed in order of their appearance in the text): Donestech, Inés Binder, Anamhoo, Acción Directa Autogestiva (ADA), Laboratorio de interconectividades y Comando Colibri, Gendersec, Florencia Goldsman, Hacks de Vida, acoso.online, EnRedadas, Derechos Digitales, Ciberfeministas Guatemala, Sula Batsú, La Imilla Hacker, Fundación Karisma, Empoderamiento de la mujer, Cl4ndestina, Luchadoras, Lucía Egaña, Chupadatos, Anamhoo, Kéfir, AnarchaServer, Vedetas

What follows is a compilation of various texts by cyberfeminists and feminists who do not regard themselves as cyberfeminists. Combining quotes from *compañeras* with one's own thoughts seems to me the best way to allow everyone to speak equally. The process of compiling this text gives me a sense of freedom. Compiling means putting together something new from what already exists, linking parts or excerpts from various texts and documents. But it is also the conversion of program code into executable code. All forms of feminism should circulate freely and inspire new actions, and cyberfeminists contribute to that by opening up new ways of disseminating information and knowledge.

Sometimes I use the first person when speaking, but generally I assume a "we." Little to nothing of what we say here is "purely" subjective. Almost everything circulates within the construction of collective practices and ideas. The stuff our dreams are made of is an incessant summoning, reading, inspiring, quoting and studying each other, conspiring and fighting together, supporting each other (and sometimes annoying and forgiving each other).

As if it were a "scene." We report from our own galaxy – with its people, collectives, and networks; with its vocabulary, codes, and languages. Situated knowledge from Latin America and beyond. All those who speak here are witnesses of violence and speak of it – violence that emerges from the criminal alliance of patriarchy and capitalism. Through sisterly love (sorority) and collaboration, we create responses to this violence; we document it, try to mitigate and thus counteract it; and last but not least, we create a feminist infrastructure among all of us.

This text describes postcolonial and cyberfeminist theories and practices. It is not only about the existing, contemporary technologies, but also about those that would be desirable and helpful but do not (yet) exist. All of the positions represented here deal with developing speculative fictions and ideas with transformative power that should not only stimulate collective actions, but also the invention of new feminist technologies.

Intro-succión[1]

Feminist theories of technology (*teorías feministas de la tecnología*, TFT) are the expression of a series of diverse and controversial social

---

1   The author plays here with the similarity of the Spanish terms *Introducción* [introduction] and *Intro-succión*, which in English would mean "sucking in."

and political movements, philosophies, and practices. What they all have in common is the goal of combating sexism and androcentrism, especially with respect to technology. Decolonial forms of feminism, on the other hand, focus on the contextualized realities of certain places and their inhabitants. They specifically address the approaches of women, gender dissidents (*disidentes de género*), non-binaries, and LGTIQs and examine their specific interactions with technology. They focus on intersectionality and criticize the ethnocentric, Western, and universalizing perspectives of many traditional TFTs. Their emphasis is to show that women constitute the main source of cheap or slave labor in the technology sector – be it in the extraction of raw materials, production, quality control, services, or writing software.

In this sense, Inés Binder asks the following question: "Can we build a postcolonial cyberfeminism that takes up the critique of cyberfeminism from the global North but, beyond that, problematizes the precariousness of infrastructures, inequality in income distribution, or racism in the Latin American region?[2]

Perhaps one of the first common, meaningful ideas of Latin American cyberfeminism emerged from the community radio environment. Inés tells us that this movement "...originated precisely here, because it placed emphasis on various demands closely linked to social movements (for example, those of alternative radio stations, citizen radio, mining radio, educational radio, guerrilla radio, popular movement radio, etc.). Although most of these radio projects were not involved in the debates about a free internet, many of them share the basic principles of cyberfeminists: freedom of expression in the broadest sense, plurality, diversity, the defense of human rights, the understanding of communication as a right and not as a commodity, the insertion of counterhegemonic discourses into the columns of the system, etc. We have even agreed to build our own infrastructure in the form of antennas and transmitters, hardware hacking, free networks, etc., and to make them more accessible."

---

2   María Inés Binder, [ciberfeministaslatam], "Identidad y agencia colectiva del movimiento ciberfeminista en América Latina" [Identity and Collective Agency in Latin America's Cyberfeminist Movement], Masters thesis in political science at the University of Salamanca, 2017. Available in Spanish: https://donestech. net/noticia/ciberfeministaslatam-investigacion-sobre-identidad-y-agencia-colectiva-del-movimiento

"We see the potential to challenge the various dimensions of power in both analog and digital communication technologies; that is why we are here, that is why we have started exactly in these places. The motto of the alternative radio station FM La Tribu is 'Apagá La Tribu y hacé tu radio' [Turn off La Tribu and create your own radio station], and today we are doing just that."[3]

But, as Inés also reminds us, sharing practices does not always mean sharing concepts, motivations, or visions: "Understanding that concepts are charged with meaning that require interpretation, putting cyberfeminism into practice necessarily entails dispute. This is the case with Latin American cyberfeminists who approached cyberfeminism through practice and not through immersion into theoretical discussions. In this sense, for the participants of [cyber feministslatam], cyberfeminism is a concept that encompasses a range of practices – from the use of technology as a tool for feminist activism, curbing sexist attacks online, and fighting the digital gender divide to creating and managing their own infrastructures based on feminist principles."[4]

And while we accept these divisions, our story will focus on common perspectives, the places where voices and ideas nourish each other, where we resonate and vibrate together like water molecules. As Anamhoo points out: "I believe that the differences in our practices are not ideological differences. We are simply in different places from where we read and create a dialectical sense of diversity. Sometimes we are very far away from each other and then again very close as far as practices and attitudes are concerned. We walk together, one with the other, looking at each other, never in parallel lines but connected, like in a net."[5]

In this sense, and as an almost intuitive response to this hostile world, we begin our story with initiatives that build self-defense projects.

---

3   Email correspondence between Inés Binder and Spideralex.

4   Ibid.

5   Email correspondence between Spideralex and Anamhoo, "Many thanks for your contribution and the revision of the text."

Feminist Self-Defense

To begin with, a statement by Acción Directa Autogestiva, ADA (Self-Managed Direct Action): "First of all, we would like to point out that self-defense is not the same as feminist self-defense. The latter consists not only of practicing a martial art, but also of creating safe spaces, collective self-care and affective networks, and of thinking about violence in all its forms and developing counter-strategies.

"Only when we can name what oppresses us, denounce it, point it out – name it again, and, most importantly, express our own desires, our dreams, our emotions, can we build something from ourselves. What is not named does not exist. ... Based on the fact that we find ourselves in a system that attacks women and everything feminine, the urgent need arises to survive and defend our life but also our joy, our self-determination, our freedom – and our collectivity.

"Feminist self-defense means staying in motion and leaving behind victimization, helplessness, and fragility. It means taking away power from these figures of thought and empowering oneself to undermine the patriarchal symbolic order. Our movement is based on collectivity, sisterhood, and connectedness. It means building a community and thus breaking through the isolation that patriarchy exposes us to in different ways, every day. It is not an easy task, but our existence depends on it. And, as we said before, we are certain that together we are stronger.

"Self-care is another fundamental axis of feminist self-defense. For centuries we have been deliberately deprived of the knowledge about our body and how it functions (now there are different movements that oppose it, such as Gynepunk in Barcelona, the midwife movement in Mexico, and the great movement for safe abortion in Latin America);[6] we were educated to care only for others; we have been formed in a culture of submission and sacrifice, causing us to always remain in the background. That is why when we say "no aggression without a response," it is part of our self-care as well. And so

---

6   As an example of cyberfeminism and supporting networks, we refer to the following research: A. Hache, M. Sanchez Martinez, "Cuerpos de mujeres en campos de batallas digitales" [Women's Bodies on the Battlefield of Digital Media], Tactical Tech, 2017. Available at: https://tacticaltech.org/media/projects/CuerposMujeres.pdf

we understand self-care as a form of resistance, as a counter-model to self-abandonment; a cry that says: "Here we are, and we want to live!" This movement serves our recovery and the protection of our spaces. It is about regaining our physical and mental strength, re-appropriating the spaces taken from us, and being able to use them freely and safely; hence the slogan: 'The street and the night belong to us.'"[7]

How do you work on feminist self-defense from a holistic perspective? How do you combine care and self-care, and how can you make better use of the power that comes from the diversity of interconnected worlds? El laboratorio de interconectividades (The Laboratory for Interconnectedness) explains it this way:

"We developed a strategic methodology of hybridizing martial arts techniques, feminist self-defense, and digital collective care. In this process, we do not distinguish between online and offline, and we work holistically, as a political commitment to the life of each and every one of us. We reconnect with our intuition, explore our bodily and spatial limits, and diagnose our daily habits in order to communicate, organize, and act more confidently and autonomously with each other."[8]

Feminist self-defense, as practiced in Latin American cyberfeminism, helps to break through the loneliness and reject the death imposed by the system. It calls for living life out of love and joy, keeping one's feet on the ground, standing firmly, and at the same time looking at the horizon, ready for the call to create other possible worlds. The situated reflection leads to a joint understanding that one can no longer think of the world as if it were marked by clear boundaries between online spaces and physical spaces. Everything is connected. Effects are greater than causes, and feedback loops have become the norm. Everything can have an impact. Everything can become relational: algorithms, objects, infrastructures, bodies, senses, emotions, data, and metadata. But you can only partially protect your life, your body, your location, your contacts, your sensitive personal data, or

7   ADA, Acción Directa Autogestiva, "Queda todo," March 2017. Available at: http://saberesyciencias.com.mx/2017/03/12/queda-todo/

8   The Autodefensas Hackfeministas [Self-Defence of Feminist Hackers] is an accomplice of the Laboratio de Interconectividades and Comando Colibri. Available at: https://lab-interconectividades.net/autodefensas-hackfeministas/, and video at: https://lab-interconectividades.net/video-autodefensas-hackfeministas-oax/

the content of your communication. There is no way to protect everything, and we all have a subjective perception and contextual security needs that change over time. We are at a stage in the history of the planet where many possible multiverses open up. At the same time, there are numerous complex questions about how we can meaningfully combine gender and intersectionality with our needs for privacy and security.

There is a place on the internet called Gendersec,[9] and some *compañeras* tell us how "this word refers to structural and systemic violence that is disproportionately directed against women and girls and other non-binary and dissident gender identities in all areas of production, access, use, development, management, and recycling of digital and electronic technologies. Actions in the face of existing violence include mutual strengthening and cooperation, solidarity and hacking, and emotional and technical assistance.

"In recent years, the internet has become an important place for women and gender dissidents to make their struggles visible, to build networks, and to develop affinities. The development of the centralized, commercial, hyper-monitored internet has led to dissident anonymous selfie actions being banned by commercial companies such as Facebook, Apple, Microsoft, and Twitter. They force users to leave their Zapatista woolen mask or the gorilla mask of the Guerrilla Girls in the closet. These developments are not accidental but the result of a neo-conservative, openly misogynistic agenda, including the disproportionate proliferation of hate groups, fanatical-religious and conservative movements that trample on human rights. They seem to

---

9   Gendersec is the wiki of the Gender and Technology Institute, which is coordinated by the Tactical Tech Collective; so far, three training programs have been implemented in Latin America in connection with Gendersec. The project is aimed at women and transgender people, activists, and human rights defenders who focus on the production of knowledge about privacy and security, as well as the implementation of care measures. The wiki documents the training activities carried out, more or less detailed (agendas, resources, motivations, feedback, and other measures). There are resources, codes, and manuals on digital security practices and tools for training and learning with others. Available at: https://gendersec.tacticaltech.org

be literally occupying the internet to carry out their violent attacks and macho practices against TODAS.[10]

"The right to be left alone has disappeared. There is no freedom of expression, only different degrees of privilege when it comes to shouting more or less loudly. The various forms of cyberfeminism resist the exodus from ICT[11] as a territory of action and create new mindscapes and narratives as well as hybrid and unexpected alliances with many other struggles."[12]

On the Move

Florencia Goldsman describes these struggles as follows:

"Latin American forms of cyberfeminism are diverse and feed on the restlessness of women and sexual dissidents who aim at politicizing the internet. They focus on practices of (digital) security and anonymity, on the streets as well as on the internet, and see this as a necessary response to the increasing militarization of our environment and our bodies. An important aspect of these forms of cyberfeminism is the continuous exchange of experiences, knowledge, and tools in self-organized workshops...

"Action has become the central political practice, and with it an awareness of inequality across the continent: while some are already technology experts, others are just beginning to learn. In any case, cyberfeminists are expanding their networks and trying to become more involved in complex and often inaccessible technology debates. We take Latin American forms of cyberfeminism as a political treasure trove for the exploration of further possibilities for freedom of expression on an internet that is becoming increasingly misogynistic. We are radicalizing our political practices and denounce paternalism, persecution, state, and corporate surveillance. Finally, we use the amplifying power of the internet to diffuse multiple narratives, to live dissent and creatively achieve more autonomy.

---

10 "TODAS" [everyone], here explicitly the plural version of the female form.

11 ICT is the acronym of the term "Information and Communications Technology."

12 The following quotes stem from a Gendersec working group on technologies of domination and have been published in a book by Ippolita that is currently only available in Italian: http://www.meltemieditore.it/catalogo/tecnologie-del-dominio/

"Exploitative companies are trying to siphon off the wealth from rivers, mines, and other natural resources in our territories, and they are in cahoots with the repressive governments of our continent. That is exactly where cyberfeminism becomes active. Everywhere, women and LGBTIQ activists fight with all sorts of means: They send out press releases from cyber cafés, use their mobile phones for political organization, borrow technical equipment, or protect themselves from the confiscation of their own infrastructure by governments (as has happened in Honduras, Nicaragua, and other countries)."[13]

Political, social, economic, ecological, and technological contexts are constantly changing. And while everything around us moves quickly, our common struggles open up new avenues. The tactical use of ICT and the internet is creating new opportunities, but it also harbors unexpected risks.

The lack of adequate measures against increasing gender-specific violence – by the operators of social platforms and by the state – has made it necessary to launch initiatives such as Acoso.online. The initiatives are "the necessary response of heterosexual women and LGBTIQ people who experience online violence on a daily basis. The digital publication of non-consensual pornography is NOT the only form of gender-based violence online.

"As you will see on the website, there is no ideal solution. Therefore, the goal of the project is not only to use the currently existing tools, but also to develop a critical sense of what could be done beyond that. In order to bring about real change, we need to use strong leverage:

- **Private internet platforms:** They must provide new policies and new tools. They must not only develop a better understanding of the complexity of non-consensual pornography and the situation of victims, but also seriously respond to their users in Latin America.

---

13 Marta Florencia Goldsman, "#libertad para belen: twitter y el debate sobre el aborto en la argentina" [#Freedom for Belen: Twitter and the Abortion Debate in Argentina], 2018. Dissertation submitted within the scope of the postgraduate program "Comunicação e Cultura Contemporâneas" at the Faculty of Communication in Bahía–UFBA as partial prerequisite for obtaining the teaching degree, with Prof. Dr. Leonor Graciela Natansohn. Available online in Spanish: https://repositorio.ufba.br/ri/handle/ri/25970

- **State:** Justice and police must stop re-victimizing people who have suffered from gender-based violence. New laws are required. The executive and legislative branches must take the problem seriously and no longer use it as a pretext for internet censorship.
- **Our Communities: Zero Tolerance of Gender Violence on the internet.** The spread of non-consensual pornography is simply unacceptable and no one should have to press charges and go to court in order to gain their rights. We demand comprehensive social ostracism.
- **Technology:** We must adopt a critical stance toward the digital technology we use. It is important to understand its functional logic as well as the business models behind it and, not least, our own role in dealing with it. As long as we do not do that, we cannot really expect much from either industry or the state."[14]

This is a cyberfeminism based on action and self-organized practices of mutual support and solidarity. Networks of women and gender dissident women are created to be there for one another and to work together against violence. Sorority!

But there is always a lack of time. And there is always a lack of resources: a lack of money, education, support, political will, and a lack of the recognition of achievements as well.

In this sense, the *compañeras* of Hacks de Vida (Hacks of Life) remind us that "it is shocking to listen to people who assist victims of gender-specific violence on the internet; the helpers are confronted with it in their own environment, in their partnerships, and in familiar safe spaces where they recognize each other. It is moving and raises many questions, because the care of people exposed to gender-based violence is largely voluntary, informal, and unpaid work.

"The fact that the supporters are feminist activists who are experienced with technology contributes to their really being able to help; they understand what can be done to remedy the violence. And it is important to point out that the ethical and moral commitment of the organizations and collectives in which these people work often does not get the recognition it deserves, either materially or otherwise.

---

14 Acoso initiative online: https://acoso.online/pornovenganza/#acerca

"In order to coordinate a common approach to gender-based violence on the internet, it is essential to better explore the phenomenon and to create the vision of a feminist future without pain and violence. The self-organization of autonomous community spaces, offline meetings, femhacks, and hackmeetings strengthens women and creates safe spaces for learning, sharing, and healing."[15]

Being Together in Free Spaces

Florencia Goldsman stresses the importance of physical encounter – the encounter of *cuerpas*[16]: "It is about meeting others[17] to spin a new world of fiber optics. For cyberfeminists, meetings are an essential part of their activities; workshops, for example, in which we learn how to use a Tor browser, or how to encrypt our emails.[18] Adult education and autodidacticism play an important role. The many experiences of personal and online encounters give rise to small initiatives, such as the production of manuals, combat kits, and self-defense instructions, which are the basis of Latin American cyberfeminist production."

In these temporary encounters in physical space, there is a kind of agreement between the *compañeras*, a mutual recognition of one another, which helps to escape the feeling of isolation. This is how they can share their experiences and views, organize workshops and concerts, work with sound, celebrate lady parties, hold cryptoparties and hackmeetings, but also write, tell stories, make films and maps, and thus contribute to building a collective memory: creating, reviving, reinterpreting, spreading, supporting, listening, informing, communicating, circulating.

In this context, the history of EnRedadas – Tecnologías para la Igualdad [Networking – Technologies for Equality] also seems

---

15 Estrella Soria and Luisa Ortiz Perez, "Enfrentan violencias de genero en América Latina" [Facing Gender Violence in Latin America], 2018. Available in Spanish at: https://archive.org/details/DocumentoHacksdeVida_201803

16 Linguistic intervention in Spanish: The male form *cuerpo* has been turned into *cuerpa* [female form], meaning the bodies of females.

17 In the Spanish version, the author uses three forms: *otras/otros y otres*, in order to include all possible gender combinations of "others."

18 There is a list of 135 activities on the Gendersec website: https://gendersec.tacticaltech.org/wiki/index.php/Category: Activities

interesting, as they strive to make these connections and networks visible. They refer here to an organization that performs a thematic mapping showing the importance of mirror games for the creation of echoes and resonances:

"For the fourth consecutive year, the Chilean NGO Derechos Digitales has produced the summary "Latin America in a Glimpse," an account of the most relevant events in Latin America in the field of technology and human rights. We are honored to have been included and invited to present it.

"This issue of 'Latin America in a Glimpse' explores the problematic and difficult relationship between gender, feminism, and the Int and presents the work of various women's groups working on this issue from this part of the world. In total, 29 initiatives from 15 Latin American countries are featured, initiatives that our friends from Dereko's Digitales find 'powerfully inspiring.'

"Among them we have included four initiatives from Central America: our outstanding FemHack, an event in which the other three initiatives from our region included in the report also participated: Ciberfeministas from Guatemala, Chicas Hacker from El Salvador, and TICas from Costa Rica. The question is how we, as Latin American women, see and live technology and the world of the internet. What we are experiencing is that in many feminist projects the question of technology is not given much importance, and in most virtual communication spaces our feminist positions are strongly rejected. As cyberfeminists, we move in both areas and actually encounter resistance and rejection everywhere."[19]

And in that same text, more cyberfeminist experiences on the internet are shared from a Latin American perspective:

"The internet, that medium that promised
us horizontal relations, mutated into
a privatized, ultra-concentrated and

---

19 EnRedadas, "Resistencia y sororidad: nuestra forma de estar en internet" [Resitance and sorority: our way of using the internet], 2017. Available in Spanish at: https://enredadasnicaragua.blogspot.com.es/2017/12/resistencia-y-sorori-dad-nuestra-forma.html

hyper-supervised environment, from which
we women are once again being excluded."
— Cyberfeminists Guatemala

"We women must create alternatives to the business
model on which the digital industry is based. We
believe that another digital economy is possible,
and that we women have the responsibility and
the opportunity to propose an alternative."
— Kemly Camacho, Sula Batsú

"When we talk about networks today, people only
think of Facebook, Twitter, and other social media.
And we are interested in disputing this term,
because networks are much more than that: they are
connections between women, dialogues, bodies."
— Lulú Barrera, Luchadoras

"The net is our loudspeaker and our balaclava."
— The Imilla Hacker

"It is clear that macho violence on and
off the internet prevents us women from
enjoying and exercising our rights fully."
— Amalia Toledo, Karisma Foundation

"Knowledge and access to technology is
still predominantly masculine and elitist,
which corroborates that women, mainly
those with limited resources, continue to
be excluded from the digital world."
— Carla and Fernanda Sánchez,
Empoderamiento de la mujer

"We want to (re)appropriate technologies,
use them in a feminist and autonomous way.
This means having control over what devices
and software we use, but it also means being

able to experiment, to make mistakes, and
not to be afraid of entering digital spaces."
– Narrira Lemos and Steffania Paola, Cl4ndestina[20]

Our network consists of interconnected spaces and personal encounters that are generally intentional and desired. But meetings are
not always possible – we do not necessarily live in the same city, often
not even in the same country, sometimes not even on the same continent. The internet can bring us very close, yes, but it is even better to meet *cuerpa*- to-*cuerpa*. The presence of the others gives us the
feeling of ecstasy, makes us float. Meeting gives us power and energy,
facilitates processes, and intensifies networks of trust and cooperation.
Sometimes we converge in our disputed territories, the street, the networks, and the servers, and other times in places where we can create
spaces of security, confidence, and relaxation. At times, we can meet
in spaces where we find safety, trust, and relaxation, but at other times
we have to venture out into contested territories, be it on the street or
the internet.

Battle Zones

The *Luchadoras* (fighters) offer a perfect place for encounters. They
know perfectly well how to connect digital and urban presence in
such a way that they reinforce each other. They define themselves as
"a feminist collective that initiates processes of political, personal,
and collective transformation in both digital and physical (public)
space and creates spaces for encounters in which women's knowledge,
strength, and power are valued, in which stories can be told and dis-
seminated, and in which a feminist-critical appropriation of technologies can be pursued.

"For the future, we imagine a world in which women, youths,
and girls can play with the potential of their personal and collective
strengths in joy and freedom in both physical and digital spaces. So
what can we do to achieve this?

"We tell stories of women warriors: We believe in the transformative
power of storytelling to combat gender stereotypes and sexism that prevail

---

20 Ibid.

in traditional media and make women feel either guilty or victimized. We tell stories of women who are capable of action, who live and/or fight for freedom and dignity. It is true that we live in the midst of a permanent war on women here in in Mexico, but we are the ones who are committed to life. In *Luchadoras* we honor everyday revolutions, stories that exist but usually remain untold. We believe that broadening the narratives expands the limits they have wanted to impose on us. It is our way of spreading what is possible – and that everything is possible!

"We work for #InternetFeminista: The internet is a public and a political space, and ICTs are tools of feminist struggle, for example by giving us access to information and claiming our rights, or by giving us means to communicate and organize ourselves. But technologies are also permeated by gender inequality, and online violence against women is growing. Through surveillance and social media conversations, we are also experiencing an increase in violence that has spread from the offline to the online world."[21]

Fanzines can also develop at these face-to-face meetings, such as, for example, "Necesito privacidad para la autonomía de mi deseo" ["I need privacy for the autonomy of my desire"]. It is the result of conversations held in a digital self-defense workshop for feminists. This fanzine stands for the desire to share some of the questions that were raised as well as possible avenues of escape – beyond that particular encounter: "Within the framework of legal regulations, which are not least also shaped by the requirements of the market, our bodies are no longer ours. Many countries enact abortion laws just as if the bodies that can reproduce were part of the (re-) productive capital of the state, a civic body so to speak, and feminists who insist on the slogan "my body belongs to me," i.e., on the opposition of mine and yours, may seem anachronistic – without really being so. But the problem is not that we should not be the sole and absolute owners of our bodies, but that others claim this exclusive ownership of our bodies. A political fantasy can therefore be to form associations that collectively manage knowledge, resources, and desires. The resistance lies in defining one's borders oneself rather than leaving it to the state, church, or multinationals."[22]

---

21 *Luchadoras*, available at: http://luchadoras.mx/que-es-luchadoras/

22 Lucía Egaña, "Me falta privacidad," [I lack privacy], in *Necesito privacidad para la autonomía de mi deseo*. Available at: https://archive.org/details/FanzineNecesitoPrivacidad

We see ourselves as a union of interconnected *cuerpas*, as a growing movement that creates unstoppable waves and entirely new alliances. Cyberfeminists who are also abortionists, defenders of the earth, hip-hoppers, anti-militarists, ecologists, artists, sex workers, researchers, poets, healers, accountants...

As life on this planet struggles not to disappear, we are creating new worlds – with speculative fiction, with radical narratives, ancestral stories, mitopoiesis, myths, and memes; autopoiesis (self-preservation and self-creation) and simptopoieisis (doing and becoming in harmony with other species).[23]

But we will still have to traverse territories in which our bodies do not belong to us; the internet: another territory to be defended; a loop, a vortex. It is as if we were always reacting; once again the feeling of losing the body, this time on the digital battlefields. Traced, monetized, discretized, objectified, analyzed, monitored, controlled, punished, violated.

Chupadatos shares with us that "as a precarious worker, as a freelancer, I have the dream of money appearing in my account with the same regularity as menstruation – every 28 days (or less). Menstruating is a very important task for the world, and now that they have discovered how to make money directly with it, it would be very good if the money would reach the pockets of those who really do the hard work of ovulation and bleeding."

In the particular case of applications aimed at controlling cycles and fertility, the perspective of unpaid work goes back to the historical lack of recognition of women's sexual, reproductive, and affective work.

In "Quantify Everything: A Dream of a Feminist Data Future," Amalia Abreu criticizes the logic and contemporary methods of quantifying life, pointing out that the advocates of this model are mostly middle and upper class men who voluntarily disclose their data. And it is precisely the same people who determine what is to be measured and how.

Although there are no fixed rules for this type of practice – it can be by means of agile applications or methodologies – worldviews are

---

23 Talk: Donna Haraway and Rosi Braidotti, Stedelijk Museum Amsterdam and Utrecht University, "On a feminist partial healing of this earth ... we always become with each other, we are simpoietic, not autopoietic, we are making with each other." Video documentation available at: https://vimeo.com/210430116

undoubtedly at play, visions that define what and why is to be measured, or who is to be measured and how. [24]

We create sanctuaries where we can go to breathe; we try to make them safe and keep them alive; refuges, places of retreat, and communities that create and maintain them. The same thing happens on the internet, where it takes the form of feminist servers, expression through the electromagnetic spectrum, community radios, and free internet connection networks. We continue to tell our stories, which resonate stronger every day, in order to preserve our freedom, to be able to decide for ourselves when we come and when we want to go, when and how we want to express ourselves in a large, beautiful, and decentralized internet; an internet where there is techno-diversity and networks of support and solidarity.

Sorry for the Inconvenience, (Feminist Infrastructure) Under Construction

Then Inés asks: "What distinguishes a cyberfeminist from a feminist who uses cyberactivism as a strategy? In general terms, cyberfeminists take a critical look at technology, understanding how it is permeated by the ideology of those who develop it: a capitalist and heteropatriarchal vision of the world.

"For example, the belief in the circulation of information in distributed networks, transparency, the collective and horizontal construction of knowledge in the hands of a community and not of actors for profit, can be translated into an individual practice such as the use of free operating systems (90 percent of those interviewed use them, of which two thirds do it exclusively) or the formation of non-hierarchical networks."[25]

---

24 Natasha Felizi and Joana Varon, "Menstruapps – ¿Cómo convertir tu menstruación en dinero (para los demás)" [Menstruapp – How Can You Turn Your Menstruation into Money (for Others)], 2016. Infographics by Diana Moreno, Natasha Felizi, and Joana Varon. Available at: https://chupadados.codingrights.org/es/menstruapps-como-transformar-sua-menstruacao-em-dinheiro-para-os-outros/

25 María Inés Binder, [ciberfeministaslatam], "Identidad y agencia colectiva del movimiento ciberfeminista en América Latina" [Identity and Collective Agengy in the Latin American Cyberfeminist Movement], 2017. A masters thesis in political science at the Univeristy of Salamanca. Available in Spanish: https://donestech.net/noticia/ciberfeministaslatam-investigacion-sobre-identidad-y-agencia-colectiva-del-movimiento

And as Laurence Rassel comments on the relationship between feminism and open source software in an interview with Donestech[26]: "In French, an operating system is called 'système d'exploitation,' so the least we can do as feminists is to own our own exploitation system and be able to modify it!"

And Anamhoo develops this idea in the following way: "If we assume that virtual space is currently subject to entrepreneurial logic, one tactic could be to use the power of consumers, but if we remain conventional consumers, we will always have to play under the terms of patriarchy. We want a 'violet revolution', and any revolution has to think about its infrastructure; return to the independent servers, the alternative social networks, which are by no means obsolete strategies. We need safe and free ways to express ourselves, we need economic and labor resources, and we need authentic networks to ensure a sustainable collaboration.

"If you still think that this is just an illusion, you need to look at projects like possibleworlds.org, rhizomatica.org, tv cherán7, or transhackfeminismo, where you can learn to administrate a feminist server. We still have a long way to go when it comes to building an infrastructure with social and feminist technologies, but at a micro-scale and in a decentralized way these possible worlds already exist as seeds of the future."[27]

Part of this feminist future are attempts to change the client-server dynamics, to write code that undoes the vertical structure of the control panel and gives more autonomy to those who inhabit it, to make words fly like butterflies, to navigate in a world of possible systems and to create friendly ways of managing our needs, Kéfir,[28] Vedetas,[29]

---

26 Documentary: "Código Lela: el día que me enrollé con las tecnologías," [LelaCode: The Day I Hooked Up with Technology], Donestech, 2007. Available at: https://www.youtube.com/watch?v=WlyFAaDsugg. See also the project LelaCoders, Interviews with cyberfeminists and hackers. Available at: http://vimeo.com/lelacoders.

27 "Oficina Antivigilancia," Anamhoo [Anti-surveillance Office], "Infraestructura para una revolución violeta" [Infrastructure for a Violet Revolution], 2016. Available at: https://antivigilancia.org/es/2016/09/infraestructura-para-una-revolucion-violeta/#sdfootnote6anc

28 See https://kefir.red/

29 See https://vedetas.org/

Codigo Sur,[30] Maddix,[31] Cl4ndestina,[32] Systerserver,[33] Matriar. cat,[34] Anarchaserver,[35] Rhizomatica,[36] Palabra radio,[37] Pi-node,[38] Tetaneutral,[39] Framasoft,[40] any many others ...

Kéfir, for example, introduces itself as follows: "A transfeminist cooperative of free technologies for activists, human rights defenders, journalists, social organizations, collectives, artists, tightrope dancers ... It is committed to co-creating digital neighborhoods where we can feel confident, express ourselves, and act without fear. We provide holistic support for the appropriation of digital technologies in community processes: from consulting to the facilitation of learning spaces, collaborative workflows for groups, online learning, and digital collective care...

"We maintain and take care of autonomous and free infrastructure on the internet. We offer a digital ecosystem based on membership: email accounts and mailing lists (encryptable), web hosting (CMS, static sites), free statistics, online archives, applications for collaborative work and calendars, voice calls, discussion and decision making forums, live streaming, project management, and e-learning platforms."[41]

Feminist servers exist as an idea, a distributed conversation, and a set of political practices that are taking place within a group of feminists and transfeminists interested in creating an autonomous infrastructure. The aim is to secure data and projects and to make accessible, preserve, and manage the experiences of feminist groups from a feminist perspective. There will be no feminist internet without autonomous feminist servers managed responsibly by their communities.

---

30 See https://codigosur.org/
31 See https://maadix.net
32 See https://clandestina.io
33 See https://systerserver.net/
34 See http://matriar.cat/
35 See http://anarchaserver.org/
36 See https://www.rhizomatica.org/
37 See https://palabraradio.org/
38 See http://p-node.org/
39 See https://tetaneutral.net/
40 See https://degooglisons-internet.org/
41 See https://Kéfir.red/

It is about regaining control and autonomy over our data, narratives, and collective memories; about having access to tools, social networks, and online services managed by feminist technology collectives or cooperatives. And, of course, it is also about advancing social and gender justice in technological environments. To achieve these goals, we need to continue discussing the following questions: What is the purpose of running a Feminist Server? What makes a server autonomous and feminist? Where are possible (socially sustainable) models for these servers? How do we build the necessary trust to develop cooperative approaches to managing these spaces of resistance and transformation?

Giving Back

We conclude this compilation of texts with some reflections by Florencia Goldsman on contemporary forms of cyberfeminism in Latin America: "A social cyberfeminism must necessarily include the vindication of the connection of different geographical regions and not just those regions that are thought to be more developed. ...

"Latin American forms of cyberfeminism constitute a network of technology activists and other active people spread across a vast continent marked by disasters, violence, emergency situations, and unequal access to ICT. In our perception as active participants in this movement, discourse arises directly from practices – not from the abstract theorization of forms of cyberfeminism.

"At present, there are still large number of open questions: How can we use technologies in a liberating way? What new instruments do we need to develop to emancipate ourselves? We work on these questions by discussing and writing together while still using spaces and tools that are determined by androcentric logic.

"The dream of a Latin American feminist internet has a necessary critical potential, but at the same time we recognize that there are already numerous initiatives with the capacity to act together and transform – without necessarily defining themselves as cyberfeminist.

"For Latin American social cyberfeminism, practiced both by women and feminists in particular, the creative appropriation of public-private technology scenarios is crucial; this in the only way to develop liberating ideas, to exercise the right to information and communication, and to make visible the demands of feminism."[42]

With all these ideas in mind and all the multiverse thinking that is yet to be discovered and produced, and knowing that this network is a galaxy that is creating new worlds, we say goodbye with the following proposals from the *compañeras* Kéfir and Vedetas:

"Our actions are not guided by the desire for more people, more women, more bodies to connect with digital technology. We accept that some will not have access to it – and may not even want to .... But we bring together different identity struggles (female, black, trans, non-binary) with a historical Latin American burden, that of being *servidoras* [servants/servers]. Against the background that we have never experienced social and economic justice, this is our way of resisting; the possibility of transgressing boundaries, of forming new alliances, and of being "servants" in a more technological sense, masters of technologies and of knowledge generated by ourselves – rather than merely reflections of what we are observing.

"Could a different design and logic create spaces that are not spaces of violence? What happens if we radically change the notion of gender, which implies that women do not create technology? What changes would we strive for at the collective level once we understand that we are not just consumers at the service of private companies? What happens when we interfere in the deepest depths of Net architecture? It is not just about gender-specific violence online, but also about designing and programming the platforms and structures that connect us. The internet could cease to be a male domain if we question the power structures that are invisible at first glance.

"It sounds utopian and far away, but in the end we are only turning back to the beginnings of the internet. We can imagine another world and also another internet, one in which we have equal rights in relation to technology; a network in which privacy and the total control of our data are fundamental principles for building safe spaces; in

---

42 Marta Florencia Goldsman, "#libertad para belen: twitter y el debate sobre el aborto en la argentina" ["#Freedom for Belen: Twitter and the Debate on Abortion in Argentina], 2018., Dissertation written as part of the post-graduate program *Comunicação e Cultura Contemporâneas* at the faculty for communication at the Federal University of Bahia.

which the same principles of autonomy apply to technology and to our bodies: our spaces, our rules, our freedom."[43]

---

43 See https://fermentos.Kéfir.red/aco-pele/ and https://www.genderit.org/node/5078.

CODES OF CONDUCT

Transforming Shared Values into Daily Practice

Femke Snelting

CODES OF CONDUCT ARE THE RULES OF BEHAVIOR THAT A COMMUNIty agrees upon. Such documents explicitly or euphemistically acknowledge the possibility of harassment, and sometimes provide guidelines for the course of action in case an incident would occur. Codes of Conduct have become default practice in Free/Libre and Open Source communities worldwide, to the point that nowadays it would be hard to find a project without one in place.[1] Projects as diverse as FreeBSD, Python, and the Free and Open source Software Developers' European Meeting (FOSDEM) have formulated protocols to address the on- and off-line behavior of their community members.

---

[1]   Geek Feminism Wiki, "Conference anti-harassment/Adoption." http://geekfeminism.wikia.com/wiki/Conference_anti-harassment/Adoption

57

In 2013, The Python Foundation asked the Libre Graphics Meeting (LGM), a community I contributed to at the time, to implement a Code of Conduct. The responses on the LGM mailing list ranged from expressions of fear that such a code might give future participants the impression that terrible things had happened, to people finding it hard to believe that Libre Graphics Meeting, an event they had always considered to be comfortable and convivial, would need a Code of Conduct to begin with. Some insisted aggressively that such codes were a preemptive response to political correctness or that "Free societies rely on open and sometimes heated public debates." Again, others worried about how the Libre Graphics Meeting Code of Conduct might contradict local laws, or wondered how negativity could be avoided: "Personally, I would like to see language that talks of 'respect' (a positive term) rather than 'anti-harassment' (a negative term)."[2] After four days of intense mailing list traffic, several people including myself volunteered to formulate a code, if only because the Python foundation had made the presence of such a document a requirement for sponsorship. For me, Codes of Conduct were part of a feminist project that confronts systemic oppression through the work of articulation. In the spirit of Jo Freeman's "Tyranny of Structurelessness."[3] I considered them a way to make discourse possible on sexism, racism, able-ism, and other forms of exclusion that operate in our communities. I joined a workgroup consisting of members from The Gimp Project, the World Wide Web Consortium, and a project that then was known as Valentina, to work on a draft and to seek consensus around it. The Libre Graphics Meeting Code of Conduct was finally adopted in 2015, but the long and confusing process that got us there left many questions unanswered.

The invitation to contribute to this publication was a welcome opportunity to work through some of the issues and challenges that Codes of Conduct present F/LOSs communities with. I started by tracing a genealogy of their appearance in the context of F/LOSs. It is an incomplete account that will hopefully invite further discussion and history writing. The essay continues with a close reading of

---

2   CREATE mailinglist, "Code of conduct," January 2014. https://lists.freedesktop. org/archives/create/2014-January/thread.html#4712

3   Freeman, Jo. "The Tyranny of Structurelessness." http://www.jofreeman.com/ joreen/tyranny.htm

eight actual documents from Python, GNOME, Ubuntu, FreeBSD, Django, KDE, Debian and, of course, the Libre Graphics Meeting. Paying attention to the phrasing of "diversity," "conflict" and "enforcement" in these documents shows how their ambitions are as dissimilar as the communities that formulate them. Now that the adoption of Codes of Conduct is ubiquitous, it seems even more important to (re-) open a conversation on their feminist potential.

The context of conduct

FLOSs communities are particularly sensitive to the ways words can be made flesh, both as code and as law.[4] The object of interest that its developers and users gather around is *source code*, a specific form of language, which is made executable through regulation. The worlding power of language is also present in the legal invention of open content licensing. By creatively turning conventional copyright law upside down, these licenses make the re-using, distribution, and development of source code possible.

While the regulatory frameworks of code and law are at its base, FLOSs communities are epistemically and culturally complex environments. The often-quoted statement "We reject: kings, presidents and voting. We believe in: rough consensus and running code,"[5] illustrates that the general spirit is anti-establishment and meritocratic. But as the projects gained in size and age, various practices of governance developed in the shape of bespoke guidelines such as the Debian Social Contract and other idiosyncratic norms, if necessary supplemented with conventional institutional forms such as the GNOME foundation, the Django Software Foundation, and the Python Foundation.

FLOSs communities have also remained predominantly white, male and Anglophone. The widely-discussed results of a large-scale

---

4 "We understand the internal perspective of legal regulation – for example, that the restrictions the law might impose on a company's freedom to pollute are a product of self-conscious regulation, reflecting values of the society imposing that regulation. That perspective is harder to recognize with code. It could be there, but it need not. And no doubt this is just one of many important differences between." Lessig, Lawrence. *Code is law.* Basic books, 2006

5 Clark, David D. "A Cloudy Crystal Ball – Visions of the Future." Presentation given at the Internet Engineering Task Force, 1992

surveys held in 2003 and 2013 helped grow awareness of the fact that Free, Libre, and Open Source communities were even less diverse than commercial software environments.[6] In the meantime, reports of harassment kept surfacing. It confirmed FLOSs communities as hostile environments where figureheads such as Richard Stallman considered it funny to make so-called "EMACS virgin jokes,"[7] where a bug-report on the presence of rote sexism in a software manual was flooded with misogynous comments,[8] and where using de-feminized IRC nicknames became a necessary strategy for many women.[9] This culture of oppressive behavior embarrassed the professional ambitions of certain projects and deeply troubled others.

It is in this paradoxical context of uncomfortable governance, of do-ocracies with a legal leaning and of normalized misogyny that Codes of Conduct emerge as the medium of choice for regulating behavior.

A genealogy of codes

Codes of Conduct come in many flavors, even if they repeat similar formulas, and go under the same name. They roughly express three interconnected but different goals: to affirm the inclusivity and diversity of FLOSS communities, to facilitate the mediation of disagreements, and to prevent and respond to cases of harassment. Some codes read as motivational mission statements, where conduct is linked to the values of the project in question. Others are more like organizational documents that emphasize the importance of efficiently resolving conflicts in order to ensure a productive environment. Again, others are explicitly formulated as anti-harassment policies.

6   "Free/Libre and Open Source Software: Survey and Study." International Institute of Infonomics University of Maastricht, The Netherlands; Berlecon Research GmbH Berlin, Germany, 2002 and "FLOSS survey 2013." Libresoft, 2013.

7   Garrett, Matthew. "RMS and virgins," 2009 https://mjg59.livejournal.com/113408.html

8   Lena. "Bug 155385 – complaint about geli(8) manpage." FreeBSD Bugzilla, 2011 https://bugs.freebsd.org/bugzilla/show_bug.cgi?id=155385

9   Meyer, Robert, Cukier, Michel. "Assessing the Attack Threat due to IRC Channels" Conference paper: Dependable Systems and Networks, 2006.

These different modes of address seem to reflect the diverse practices that implicitly or explicitly influenced the formulation and (imagined) function of Codes of Conduct in the context of FLOSS. Historically, the term "Code of Conduct" appears in relation to the changing international business practices in the early 1990s. In the aftermath of state de-regulation and the globalization of capital, transnational companies were pressured by NGOs and trade unions to voluntary adopt Codes of Conduct. In the absence of state control and international legal frameworks, this would, at least in theory, regulate the impact of global enterprises on social and environmental conditions.[10] It is no surprise that the de-politicized mix of managerial and motivational language of these business codes rings through in documents adopted by projects such as Ubuntu and Python. Both projects operate in a US-based entrepreneurial environment.

A second influence is the informal tradition of "netiquette," which circulated in the early days of the Internet. Reiterating the way "etiquette" functions as a framework to govern social interactions through behavioral norms, netiquette established a loose set of conventions, which facilitated friction-free interaction over networks.[11] Commonsense advice such as "Remember that the recipient (of your e-mail) is a human being whose culture, language, and humor have different points of reference from your own," has found its way into many Codes of Conduct.

In some codes, for example the one for GNOME and Ubuntu, you can recognize the ambition of traditional oaths such as The Order of the Engineer or the Hippocratic Oath that medical students pledge before entering professional life. In a similar fashion, Ubuntu requires new contributors to electronically undersign their Code of Conduct as part of a rite of passage into the Ubuntu community.

Last but not least, Codes of Conduct are influenced by feminist and LGBTQ activism for Safe Spaces, as well as anti-oppression practices that address racism, sexism, homophobia, and trans-phobia

---

10 Jenkins, Rhys. "Corporate Codes of Conduct: Self-Regulation in a Global Economy." UNRISD Programme Papers on Technology, Business and Society, 2001.

11 The Internet Engineering Task Force (IETF), "Netiquette Guidelines." https://tools.ietf.org/html/rfc1855

head on.[12] Their intersectional approach to privilege and power can be found in the language and methods of certain Codes of Conduct, such as the one adopted by FreeBSD. This influence can be partially traced back to the persistence of the US-based Ada Initiative that, in the period 2011-2015, actively interfered with the internal politics of many FLOSS projects in order to make sure they would adopt effective Codes of Conduct.

The first code in the context of FLOSS appeared in 2004. Debian and Ubuntu contributor Benjamin Mako Hill allegedly typed up "one of the key innovations that Ubuntu pioneered in free software communities" over lunch.[13] In the rationale for this casual innovation, Ubuntu explains that the code is the foundation for all of their governance practices and should "help people participate in decisions regarding the Ubuntu community and distribution."[14] Due to its early arrival in a widespread community, and maybe because of the exclusively positive terminology it uses, this document has served as a template for many codes to follow.

It took almost ten years before the adoption of CoCs spread wider. From 2008 onwards, contributors to The Geek Feminism Wiki actively documented harassment in the context of FLOSS, the technology industry, gaming, and fandom. They were joined by the Ada Initiative in 2011, and their combined efforts have no doubt had an important influence on the sense of urgency that especially US-based projects must have felt.[15] Ada Initiative founder Mary Gardiner explains: "Had you asked me in 2003 for troublesome incidents in Free Software... I don't know that I would have been able to give you examples of anyone doing anything much wrong. A few unfortunate comments about cooking and babies at LUGs, perhaps. Things started to change my awareness slowly."[16] In 2014, a growing number of

---

12 Fithian, Lisa, Oswald Mitchell, Dave. "Theory: Anti-oppression" in: *Beautiful Trouble*, OR books, 2012.

13 Mako Hill, Benjamin. "Updating the Ubuntu Code of Conduct." https://mako.cc/copyrighteous/updating-the-ubuntu-code-of-conduct

14 "Governance." Ubuntu website. https://www.ubuntu.com/community/governance

15 "Timeline of Incidents." Geek Feminism Wiki. http://geekfeminism.wikia.com/wiki/Timeline_of_incidents

16 Gardiner, Mary. "Why we document." *Geek Feminism Blog*, 2009 https://geekfeminism.org/2009/08/19/why-we-document

conference organizers and speakers began to pledge that they would stop contributing to events without a Code of Conduct in place,[17] and both the Python and the Django foundation demanded all projects they sponsored to adopt a Code of Conduct. By this time, social and financial pressure had aligned to normalize Codes of Conduct even for the most reluctant communities.

Gaining strength from diversity

Reading through the Codes of Conduct of seven major FLOSS communities (Python, GNOME, Ubuntu, FreeBSD, Django, KDE and Debian) and the Libre Graphics Meeting, it is striking how many of them open with a diversity statement:

> "The Python community is made up of members from around the globe with a diverse set of skills, personalities, and experiences. It is through these differences that our community experiences great successes and continued growth." (Python)

The TODO Group, an initiative that developed the influential Open Code of Conduct, believes that the adoption of a code helps "set the ground rules for participation in communities, and more importantly helps to build a culture of respect and improve diversity."[18] With the majority of FLOSS contributors being white, male, and from the affluent North,[19] this imagined "diversity" is still sadly at odds with reality. Explicitly articulating diversity in a Code of Conduct can be part of a strategy to change the culture from within and might have an effect on diversification in the long term. It is also

---

17 #cocpledge https://twitter.com/cocpledge

18 TODO. "Open Code of Conduct" https://github.com/todogroup/ opencodeofconduct/tree/13611b3023881dbf5a2914e73873dea178e160fc

19 Demby, Gene. "Why Isn't Open Source a Gateway For Coders Of Color?" *Code Switch*, December 2013 https://www.npr.org/sections/ codeswitch/2013/12/05/248791579/why-isnt-open-source-a-gateway-for-coders-of-color. Dryden, Ashe. "The Ethics of Unpaid Labor and the OSS Community." https://www.ashedryden.com/blog/the-ethics-of-unpaid-labor-and-the-oss-community

fair to say that Ubuntu, Debian, and Python have not only adopted a Code of Conduct, but also initiated multiple activities and policies to address gender disparity in their communities.

> "We gain strength from diversity, and actively seek participation from those who enhance it. This code of conduct exists to ensure that diverse groups collaborate to mutual advantage and enjoyment. We will challenge prejudice that could jeopardise the participation of any person in the project." (Ubuntu)

However, such hopeful diversity statements run the risk of obscuring the systemic problems operating within and around these projects. The insistence on being already inclusive might make it harder to report incidents that would contradict such claims: "Diversity provides a positive, shiny image of the organization that allows inequalities to be concealed and thus reproduced."[20]

Other uses of the term "diversity" address differences within the relatively homogeneous but internationally distributed communities of FLOSS, where proud autodidacts, opinionated computer scientists, engineering students, hobbyists, and professionals gather. To communicate in many flavors of English across varying social and cultural backgrounds can be challenging:

> "Diversity is one of our huge strengths, but it can also lead to communication issues and unhappiness. To that end, we have a few ground rules that we ask people to adhere to." (Django)

> "We accept that people have differences of opinion, that they communicate those in various ways, and that social norms may vary across cultures. Sometimes the impact our behaviour has on others isn't immediately apparent to us." (Libre Graphics Meeting)

---

20 Ahmed, Sarah. *On Being Included: Racism and Diversity in Institutional Life.* Duke University Press, 2012.

The acknowledgment of "communication issues" hints at the cost of conflict that can paralyze development more than anything. It becomes clear that Codes of Conduct not only express a desire for diversity but also propose ways to manage the flow of collaboration in order to secure a productive environment:

> "Debian contributors have many ways of reaching our common goal of a free operating system which may differ from your ways. Assume that other people are working towards this goal. Note that many of our contributors are not native English speakers or may have different cultural backgrounds." (Debian)

> "The FreeBSD Project is inclusive. We want the FreeBSD Project to be a venue where people of all backgrounds can work together to make the best operating system, built by a strong community." (FreeBSD)

Conflict resolution for healthy communities

Techno-ideological conflicts in FLOSs environments can be relentless. These "disagreements" prove hard to resolve on the basis of meritocratic values such as technical excellence, effort, or achievement alone. Because conflicts can paralyze projects for long periods of time, it became important to develop practices that prevent the costly re-negotiation of core aims as much as possible.[21] It is telling that even Linus Torvalds, notorious for testing the limits of conduct himself,[22] decided to merge a "Code of Conflict" into the Linux Kernel documentation:

> "In a project the size of Debian, inevitably there will be people with whom you may disagree, or find it difficult to cooperate. Accept that, but even so, remain

---

21 Mateos-Garcia, Juan, Steinmueller, W. Edward. "The Institutions of Open Source Software: Examining the Debian Community" in: *Information Economics and Policy* Volume 20, Issue 4, December 2008, Pages 333-344

22 Corbet, Jonathan. "How to enforce Debian's code of conduct." lwn.net, September 2012 https://lwn.net/Articles/611317/

respectful. Disagreement is no excuse for poor behavior or personal attacks, and a community in which people feel threatened is not a healthy community." (Debian)[23]

In the "'socially-light' and 'intimacy-averse'"[24] on-line environments of IRC channels and mailing lists, a disagreement can easily turn into a development-crippling flame-war. In their respective codes, the Django and KDE project carefully formulate their idea of constructive conduct in such case:

"Disagreements, both social and technical, happen all the time and Django is no exception. It is important that we resolve disagreements and differing views constructively. Remember that we're different." (Django)

"Disagreements, both political and technical, happen all the time. Our community is no exception to the rule. The goal is not to avoid disagreements or differing views but to resolve them constructively." (KDE)

Dealing with the consequences

All documents but one (Debian has published a separate diversity statement) highlight the diversity and inclusiveness of their respective communities, and all but one (FreeBSD) pay attention to how disagreements should be dealt with. The prevention of, and response to harassment receives much less attention, arrives at the end of the documents and is often not present at all.

The priorities of the Ada Initiative clearly lie elsewhere. According to them, an effective Code of Conduct includes, first of all, "Specific descriptions of common but unacceptable behavior (sexist jokes,

---

23 Linux Kernel Documentation Code of Conflict https://www.kernel.org/doc/html/v4.10/process/code-of-conflict.html

24 *The institutions of Open Source Software: Examining the Debian Community*, Mateos-Garcia, Juan, Steinmueller, W. Edward. "The Institutions of Open Source Software: Examining the Debian Community" in: *Information Economics and Policy* Volume 20, Issue 4, December 2008, Pages 333-344

etc.)" and, additionally, "reporting instructions with contact information, information about how it may be enforced, a clear demarcation between unacceptable behavior (...) and community guidelines such as general disagreement resolution." According to a survey on the Geek Feminism Wiki, not many Codes of Conduct fulfill these first three requirements:

> "Overall, we're good to each other. We contribute to this community not because we have to, but because we want to. If we remember that, these guidelines will come naturally." (Python)[25]

The insistence of the Ada Initiative on enforceable mechanisms of responsibility comes down to two basic elements: listing unacceptable behavior takes away the burden from someone reporting harassment to define the nature of harassment itself, and clear guidelines will guarantee that in case something happens, those who report incidents can trust that they will be heard.

When it comes to enforcement, some codes assume that guidelines lead to better conduct naturally. Others explicitly state that their Code of Conduct will not be enforced:

> "GNOME creates software for a better world. We achieve this by behaving well towards each other. Therefore this document suggests what we consider ideal behavior, so you know what to expect when getting involved in GNOME. This is who we are and what we want to be. There is no official enforcement of these principles, and this should not be interpreted like a legal document." (GNOME)

The phrase "this should not be interpreted like a legal document" points to the complicated relation that these codes have with the law. It seems, at least partially, related to the reluctance to summon external governing bodies, unless absolutely necessary:

---

25 "Code of conduct evaluations." Geek Feminism Wiki http://geekfeminism.wikia. com/wiki/Code_of_conduct_evaluations

> "If you believe anyone is in physical danger, please no-
> tify appropriate law enforcement first." (FreeBSD)

Communication on mailing lists happens between geographically
dispersed participants, so it is not always clear which local laws apply.
For conferences, it might be that the legal situation of a host country
does or does not cover the terms specified in the code. In many cases, anti-discrimination statements reiterate international and national
agreements as if they are community-specific values:

> "To achieve the goals of the Code of Conduct, the or-
> ganizers of the Libre Graphics Meeting will check be-
> fore the selection of a location is made, if local laws are
> compatible with the CoC." (Libre Graphics Meeting)

Whenever a Code of Conduct includes a clause with reporting
instructions and ways the code may be enforced, this comes down
to assigning specific community members as "community liaison" or
"Code of Conduct Committee." They are charged with information
gathering, deciding whether a violation was committed, and carrying
out a sentence if applicable. This can be a private or public repri-
mand, a permanent or temporary ban, a request for public or private apology or a process of mediation. As a consequence, the way
community-members relate to each other radically changes. Not en-
forcing a Code of Conduct that promises to do so is alienating for
those experiencing or reporting a violation. But when some volunteer
members become responsible for policing others, this can create difficult and destabilizing situations for everyone involved: reporters of
harassment, perpetrators of violations, and liaisons alike. There is no
easy way out:

> "We will do our best to respond within one week to
> the person who filed the report with either a resolu-
> tion or an explanation of why the situation is not yet
> resolved. Once we have determined our final action,
> we will contact the original reporter to let them know
> what action (if any) we will be taking." (FreeBSD)

"The contact person(s) will take appropriate measures when necessary, such as removing someone from the premises or channels." (Libre Graphics Meeting)

Only two of the eight documents that I worked with demarcate unacceptable behavior. Django lists desired conduct first (be respectful, considerate, collaborative, open, patient, generous, assume people mean well, take responsibility...) before arriving at the following definition:

"Violent threats or language directed against another person. Discriminatory jokes and language. Posting sexually explicit or violent material. Posting (or threatening to post) other people's personally identifying information ("doxing"). Personal insults, especially those using racist or sexist terms. Unwelcome sexual attention. Advocating for, or encouraging, any of the above behavior. Repeated harassment of others. In general, if someone asks you to stop, then stop." (Django)

Such dictionaries of harassment are painful to write and read. But as intersectional activist Lisa Fithian warns us, the discomfort comes with facing oppression and is a necessary part of the process:

"Comments that reinforce systemic oppression related to gender, gender identity and expression, sexual orientation, disability, mental illness, neurodiversity, physical appearance, body size, age, race, or religion. Unwelcome comments regarding a person's lifestyle choices and practices, including those related to food, health, parenting, drugs, and employment. Deliberate misgendering. Deliberate use of "dead" or rejected names. Gratuitous or off-topic sexual images or behavior in spaces where they're not appropriate. Physical contact and simulated physical contact (e.g. textual descriptions like "*hug*" or "*backrub*") without consent or after a request to stop. Threats of violence. Incitement of violence towards any individual, including encouraging a person to commit suicide or to engage in self-harm. Deliberate intimidation. Stalking or following. Harassing photography or recording, including logging online activity for harassment purposes. Sustained disruption of discussion. Unwelcome sexual attention. Pattern of inappropriate social contact, such as requesting/assuming inappropriate levels of intimacy with others. Continued one-on-one communication after requests to cease. Deliberate "outing" of any private aspect of a person's identity without their consent except as necessary to protect vulnerable people from intentional abuse. Publication of non-harassing private communication without consent. Publication of non-harassing private communication with consent but in a way that intentionally misrepresents the communication (e.g. removes context that changes the meaning). Knowingly making harmful false claims about a person." (FreeBSD)[26]

The feminist potential of Codes of Conduct

Now that many FLOSs projects have adopted Codes of Conduct, the attention for these documents rapidly diminishes. The Ada Initiative closed in 2015, the Geek Feminism wiki is currently in archive mode, and TODO announced that it "will not be continuing work on the open code of conduct."[27] The Code of Conduct adopted by the Libre

26 Fithian, Lisa, Oswald Mitchell, Dave. "Theory: Anti-oppression" in: *Beautiful Trouble*, OR books, 2012.

27 Ada-Initiative. "The Ada Initiative closed in October 2015 but we encourage you to continue supporting women in open technology and culture by continuing and building on the Ada Initiative's work." https://adainitiative.org/2015/08/announcing-the-shutdown-of-the-ada-initiative/ Geek Feminism Wiki. "The Geek Feminism Wiki is effectively in archival mode. New accounts are restricted from editing due to vandalism, and we do not have the volunteer labor available to whitelist new accounts and monitor activity" http://geekfeminism.wikia.com/wiki/Geek_Feminism_Wiki TODO. "Update: We will not be continuing work on the open code of conduct." http://todogroup.org/opencodeofconduct/#Open+Code+of+Conduct

Graphics Community in 2015 has never been evaluated, adjusted, or discussed afterwards.

Obviously there are a lot of questions to ask about the ways in which these codes really function. Do the communities that adopt them indeed diversify? Did the amount of disagreements diminish, and were they dealt with more constructively? Are there fewer incidents of harassment to report? And have communities gotten better at handling incidents?

I think there is feminist potential hidden in the meticulous but confused wordings of Codes of Conduct. The process of formulating them provided a much-needed platform for community-wide conversations on harassment and mechanisms of exclusion. Codes that contain explicit examples of harassment have made people reflect on their own contribution to the pervasiveness of oppressive behavior, even if reluctantly and awkwardly. They have opened up the possibility to identify and call out such behavior and have made it clear that there exists relentless resistance to do so as well. When it comes to enforcement, I wonder about the way projects seem to agree on trusting dedicated community members with the task. It means essentially a move of containment that makes it very hard to address these issues beyond individual perpetration. We might learn from radical feminist hacker-initiatives how to build collective spaces that allow us to address systemic oppression together.

Without collective attention and experimentation, Codes of Conduct risk producing a sense of already-safe and already-diverse environments where diversity work is efficiently outsourced to the document. We need to keep activating these tools to articulate concerns and to create communities of conduct that can operate with difference, that can keep conflict in the room, and that are ready to work through mistakes. We should abandon these documents. They deserve our persistent interaction and intervention.

Bibliography

This text is based on a close reading of the following Codes of Conduct:

- FreeBSD https://www.freebsd.org/internal/code-of-conduct.html
- Debian https://www.debian.org/code_of_conduct
- Ubuntu https://www.ubuntu.com/community/code-of-conduct

- Libre Graphics Meeting https://libregraphicsmeeting.org/lgm/public-documentation/code-of-conduct/
- KDE https://www.kde.org/code-of-conduct/
- Django https://www.djangoproject.com/conduct/
- GNOME https://wiki.gnome.org/action/show/Foundation/CodeOfConduct
- Python https://www.python.org/psf/codeofconduct/

THE FEMINIST PRINCIPLES OF THE INTERNET

or the personal_collective story of
imagining and making #feministinternet

Text by hvale vale

Intro

Creation, except in religious stories, is never an act of loneliness or solitude. Creation is the transcendence of the personal in a voluntary recognition of the shared purpose of a journey.

I could have said this using one word: feminism. But then I would have spent far more time explaining what feminism, and which feminists I might mean by that. So, I thought, let's start from co-creation and pleasure before going into the long, arcane labor of building communities, opening/discovering paths takenby activists in their local, embodied resistances, push-backs, and hopes for a diversity-welcoming world.

Feminist principles are born in and from the political thinking of an incredible group of 52 activists from various realms: women's rights, sexuality, digital/internet rights, and intersectional feminism. The personal and collective space of *r_existence*[1] is overwhelmingly what in international development jargon is called the "Global South," meaning the entire world except the Northern-Western-white-capitalist-male: North America, the EU, Australia, and New Zealand. Having said that, since each North needs to have a South to threaten, among those 52 feminists there were activists born and coming from the abovementioned North.

Beyond traditional geography, the most prominent territorial dimension of feminist principles is the internet. Understanding the internet and its digital, virtual dimension as intrinsically the same *s_place*[2] in hosting our lives, is essential to understanding the "why" of the Feminist Principles of the Internet.

The internet hosts a continuum of our bodies, not a fractured or fragmented projection of data bits. The internet is in fact just another dimension of the world we all live in. As such, it flourishes with exclusions, exploitations, misogyny, sexism, racism… and flourishes with creation, passion, and of course, hacking.

So, the story of the Feminist Principles of the Internet is a story of co-creation: the perpetual, collective, and passionate hacking. I will try to tell this story from the beginning, as I know it.

Questions from Cornelia Sollfrank
Answers by hvale vale

CS: *You have been involved in the process of writing up the Feminist Principles of the Internet.*

First of all, could you please explain what these principles are, or give a general description/overview.

HV: The Feminist Principles of the Internet are a compass to help us move through the uncharted and wild territory of the *InternetS* (we'll

---

1   Neologism coined by the author, combining the words "resistance" and "existence," indicating the attitude of resisting through everyday life.

2   Neologism coined by the author combining the words "space" and "place."

come back later to the plural), and at the same time, the drawing of that territory, i.e. the chart itself.

The Feminist Principles of the Internet are a political and analytical framework. They offer a perspective that comes from the lived experience of "women and queer persons in all our diversities." A reading that embeds the theoretical and the programmatic in a nutshell. As co-creation, it changes through the experiences, reflections, and conversations of the persons that participated and have become part of them. The current version of the Feminist Principles of the Internet (FPIs) consists of 17 principles, which can be grouped into five broad areas/sections: Access, (Principles 1, 2, and 3); Movements and Public Participation, (Principles 4, 5, and 5); Economy (Principles 7 and 8); Expression (Principles 9, 10, and 11); and Embodiment (Principles 12, 13, 14, 15, 16, and 17).

The first, Access, comprises of multiple dimensions: from connectivity, cables and last miles, to devices, content, and the ability to access information, but also to produce and share it. It speaks of autonomous infrastructures, decentralized networks owned by people, and of the many potential InternetS against the one-size-fits-all-internet promoted by corporations.

The principles regarding Movement and Public Participation recognize the internet as a place and a space of public discourse, and as such, our space of resistance and transformation. A space of resistance against the oppressive and discriminatory social norms, but also a space of power and creativity used to connect and build movement from the very local to the very global. It states that technology is a given in our movement building and calls for understanding the machine and reclaiming it down to the code.

This concept is then expanded and explained throughout the principles regarding Economy and Open Source, which touch upon the economic model and its roots. It envisions an economy based on solidarity and denounces the exploitative nature of the various venture start-ups. It talks about collective intelligence, the right to see, build, and change the code, but also about a different concept of security – one that is centered on people rather than states.

The next thematic area under the theme Expression introduces counter-narratives and bodies as expression that counters the traditional discourse of freedom of speech based on ideas and words. It touches on pornography, but also "harmful" content and links it to agency, consent, labor, and power.

The last set of principles is all about Embodiment and like the rest, is entrenched in feminist analyses, its practices, and the multiple discriminations it contends with. Each and every principle is based on intersectionality and these last six principles complete the framework. Consent: Yes means yes, and no means no – there isn't any room for a blank yes; no predatory tick that can be made, and that stands for consent regarding unclear and constantly changing terms of use. The principle of Consent is theorized and practiced by feminism to explain gender-based violence. It has to be explicit, meaningful, and informed. The next one focuses on the intersection of data and privacy, far preceding the GDPR (the EU's General Data and Protection Regulation). This is followed by Memory as the cornerstone of building and growing personal and collective stories, and echoing the many archives and the incredible efforts that bring visibility to all voices and all personal stories. The last three principles regarding Anonymity, Children and Youth, and Online Violence close this thematic area. Their sequence is not accidental. The Feminist Principles project aims at dismantling patriarchy. This entails heteronormativity, gender identity, sexual taboos, and social norms that are enforced online through the powerful algorithm full of internalized and undisclosed bias.

Each of the principles recognizes the challenges and does not give black and white, or binary solutions. Instead, they call for agency and recognition of diversity. That's why online violence appears last. The bodies that are targeted, our bodies, are targeted because of the ways in which *they-are-not*.

Online violence is the product of a misogynistic, patriarchal, moralistic world and because of this, access to the internet is prevented – a vicious circle of cause and effect.

The principles are by their nature short statements. They mention the change, how the world would look like with, and on, a feminist internet. They are a vision. When reading or using them, there is no need to take them as an indivisible block.

They come from activists, from the women's rights, sexual rights, and internet rights movements. They came into existence as an act of freedom and with the intention to give form to the shared desire for a feminist internet in our practices of resistance and transformation.

We have all experienced the mainstream assumption of the neutrality of the internet/technology, invariably used to invalidate any request for participation, accountability, transparency, and response that linked the internet to issues of gender, sexuality, class, race, disability, and so on. The invisibility cloak that was covering all our bodies was the norm of the internet/technology.

We need to look at the principles as an exercise of naming the territory called "the internet" from a feminist perspective. And I say "territory" because we did not look at the internet as a tool, but as a space, a place not unlike the other places and spaces in which activists and feminists invest their lives to achieve change, justice, and transformation.

We also wanted to build an instrument to help dismantle the assumptions coming from the "neutral" minds and bodies. A chart that would call out this embodiment as part of the patriarchy and its "assumption of neutrality" as the "absence of self-reflection on genders, sexualities and power." So the Feminist Principles of the Internet are part of the "herstorical" production of a feminist manifesto that signifies knowledge and a political stand. As such they are short, dense, affirmative, and open.

A clarification: I use "we" as an open-ended collective of people. The experience around the FPI was and is collective, and what I am describing here is how I came to be a part of it, who called me in, and why I feel strongly about the FPI. The FPI were and are a process started in 2014[3] and the current version was finalized in 2016.

CS: *How did the idea emerge to create such a document, who was involved in producing it and could u please describe some milestones of this process?*

HV: The first version of the FPI was drafted in Malaysia in April 2014, during "Imagine a Feminist Internet," an event attended by more than 50 activists organized by the Association for Progressive Communication (APC). The conveners of the Feminist Principles of the Internet were the incredible, visionary intersectional feminists and activists from the Women's Rights Program[4] of APC in 2014.

---

3   See   https://www.genderit.org/articles/plain-sight-sexuality-rights-and-internet-india-nepal-and-sri-lanka

4   See https://www.apc.org/about/people/staff

The following year another meeting took place and in 2016 the current version of the FPIs was published. The FPI version 1.0[5] and 2.0[6] are the result of many conversations, in many languages, held locally and globally. Reflections and knowledges that feed back to each other in an environment of trust. Trust in the conveners, trust in the process, trust in the persons holding the process, trust in the community.

If I have to think of the start, I cannot give a precise date. I know that the FPI are the result of many years of advocacy and knowledge-building by activists and feminists engaged at the intersection of many networks and movements: women's rights, sexual rights and digital rights movements that wanted to articulate their actions, strategy and politics and build a language that recognizes the issue of power[7] and could be used to enhance the transformative power of internet and technology. An open call for an internet of rights, pleasure, and social justice. An internet that would recognize the discrimination it produces and expand and work to end it. An internet focused and centered on people, their realities, and diversity.

From this desire, the politics of solidarity, embodiment, and trust have emerged. My story is just one version of what happened, and for people that want to know more I would suggest they look at the Feminist Internet online platform, or browse the internet to reach out to activists and friends.

CS: *How big was the group involved in the discussion and production process, and what are the contexts and backgrounds of the people involved?*

HV: More than 100 people participated in drafting the current version of the FPI during the two global meetings in 2014 and 2015, but many more used, critiqued, translated, and tested them into the form they have now. Last year, a third global assembly with approximately 80 activists moved from "Imagine a Feminist Internet" to "Make a

---

5   See https://www.genderit.org/sites/default/upload/fpi_v3.pdf

6   See https://feministinternet.org/en

7   See   https://www.genderit.org/feminist-talk/panel-power-politics-and-agency-imagineafeministinternet

Feminist Internet"[8]: that is, movement-building in the digital age, because as I said, the feminist internet proceeds by iterations.

CS: *You are using the first person plural, "we," in the document. Who can consider themselves to belong to this "we" and who does not?*

HV: The principles speak to different realities: age, disabilities, sexualities, gender identities and expression, socioeconomic locations, political and religious beliefs, and racial markers. So I would say, anyone who senses the "we" as part of the self is part of it! Whoever is willing to engage in the transformative power of feminism. The catch is that it is inclusive, not exclusive, candid about privilege. So I would say the "we" is open, is the self/selves that need to reflect and make the move toward it.

CS: *What were the most interesting/challenging aspects in the process of discussion?*

HV: Putting together movements, politics, practices. Acknowledging the diversities and the privileges. Staying open and flexible, but also firm and clear. For me, the FPI talk about power. The power we challenge and dismantle and the power we have, we share, we transform. Conversations about power are always challenging. Usually, we - the "we" I refer – see power used against us, but power asks for an intimate reflection. It is about understanding the place from where each of us speaks. The interesting part – and I think the fascination of the FPI – is that they are embodied by the people and this makes them absolutely fascinating and constantly evolving. To capture a vision of the world (the #feministinternet) in 17 principles is quite an exercise. The smile, the focus, the care, the passion enfolded in a welcoming-of-each-and-everyone-ethic is what makes the FPIs special. They come from the lived experience of many activists. They are not a theoretical exercise, but they embed theory – a lot. They are a community and a platform. They are inscribed in the digital age. They come from and to the internet, and from and to our bodies. They are emotions and pleasure, but also justice and rights.

---

8   See https://www.genderit.org/edition/making-feminist-internet

CS: *What is it that you have learned personally while working with the others on the document?*

HV: Well, the Feminist Internet was a blast, and in my best political feeling, the best feminism I have ever practiced. The joy, the pleasure, the intimacy, the commitment, the passion that permeated the first meeting was the same that I felt in many other moments, instances, places. It sits with very specific people, activists I knew or met and resonated with, whether it was a digital story-telling workshop or a conference, or an internet governance forum. In any of those places, I was not alone and we had a very similar language, same sense, and same politics. So, when the #feministinternet meme surfaced, it just resonated and kept growing, and I sense it was a turning point. I arrived at the first Imagine a Feminist Internet with no expectation but full commitment. I only knew that it would be a place of joy. I did not become an activist to suffer, but to transform. I was convened, but felt like one of the conveners, and it is really special when the ones being hosted feel as if they are hosting also. There are many conventions and often they regard the branding as intrinsic. The FPIs did not, because the embodied feminist queer politics of the people that worked to run the #ImagineaFeministInternet, at Women's Rights Program of APC, is so strong that it is far beyond the little greedy gardens of the many initiatives preoccupied with their status rather than transformation. The FPI are one of my vital spaces for co-creation. My learning is from being one of many, knowing how each and every contribution is essential – just as listening is essential and living is essential, and continuing is essential. And as a feminist, I'd like to thank the people that brought me there to transform.

CS: *Where and how (locally and online) did the discussions take place? Was there a moderator involved or was the process self-organized?*

HV: The conversations are continuous. The principles belong to anyone and we encourage people to use them locally, online as well as offline. This form embraces talks, workshops. They are there to help the discussion of issues related to our lives and the internet/technology and to help explore how they relate to specific contexts and realities. We know of some conversations, but there are many that just happen, and we/I learn about them casually. I would say that as a co-creation exercise, it is important to share the learning and the reflection because in this way the Feminist Principles continue to grow, transform themselves and anyone who is interested and feels part of this conversation. To help this two-way communication, it is best to visit our website, there are some suggestions and a contact email.[9] Anyone, individually or as a collective, can contribute to a principle. People can register and contribute through stories, ideas, and actions. Or, one can host a City Conversation "to adapt, localize and grow the FPI's" in a sort of spiral learning that always comes back to itself, but at a different level, similar but never the same, enriched and transformed by a repetition articulated locally and as a result of this diversity. The aim – and I will quote from the platform – is: "(...) to build a cross-movement interaction between sexual rights, women's rights and internet rights activists, to strengthen participation in internet policy processes, as well as deepen discussions specifically around privacy, the right to information and freedom of expression from a feminist and gender justice perspective."

CS: *How important is it to you to have the document available in many languages and how to do you make the document known? (For example, in the academic/art context that I am active in, nobody has heard of the document before.)*

HV: The simple fact of translation generates reflection, conversation, discussion, and knowledge. There are more than 6,500 languages in the world. Very few people speak some, but for example Mandarin Chinese, is spoken by close to 850 million people in the world. So, yes, languages are important. We are aware that due to their position of power, English and Spanish have a huge base of secondary speakers. So we used English and Spanish as bridge languages, being aware of the intrinsic colonialist, imperialist pattern embedded in them. We invite people to translate the Feminist Principles of the Internet into their own languages, because during the process of translation inconsistencies and specificities will emerge. The current thematic area of "Embodiment" was previously "Agency," which is a concept that doesn't translate directly into many languages. I remember our own process while translating into BCS (Bosnian-Croatian-Serbian).

---

9   See https://feministinternet.org/en/about

So, languages are part of the conversation as explicitly mentioned in Principle 2: "Access to information - We support and protect unrestricted access to information relevant to women and queer persons, particularly information on sexual and reproductive health and rights, pleasure, safe abortion, access to justice, and LGBTIQ issues. This includes diversity in languages, abilities, interests and contexts."

CS: *Whom does the document address? Ideally, what would you like to achieve?*

HV: Anyone who recognizes herself/himself/themselves as a feminist and anyone who wants to engage in pleasure, play, and the dismantling of patriarchy.

FEMINIST PRINCIPLES OF THE INTERNET – VERSION 2.0

Author: Association for Progressive Communication APC

Publication date: August 2016

Available at: https://www.apc.org/en/pubs/
feminist-principles-internet-version-20

Preamble

A FEMINIST INTERNET WORKS TOWARDS EMPOWERING MORE WOMEN and queer persons – in all our diversities – to fully enjoy our rights, engage in pleasure and play, and dismantle patriarchy. This integrates our different realities, contexts, and specificities – including age, disabilities, sexualities, gender identities and expressions, socioeconomic locations, political and religious beliefs, ethnic origins, and racial markers. The following key principles are critical towards realizing a feminist Internet.

Access

1. Access to the Internet
A feminist Internet starts with enabling more women and queer persons to enjoy universal, acceptable, affordable, unconditional, open, meaningful, and equal access to the internet.

2. Access to information
We support and protect unrestricted access to information relevant to women and queer persons, particularly information on sexual and reproductive health and rights, pleasure, safe abortion, access to justice, and LGBTIQ issues. This includes diversity in languages, abilities, interests, and contexts.

3. Use of technology
Women and queer persons have the right to code, design, adapt and critically and sustainably use ICTs and reclaim technology as a platform for creativity and expression, as well as to challenge the cultures of sexism and discrimination in all spaces.

Movements and public participation

4. Resistance
The internet is a space where social norms are negotiated, performed and imposed, often in an extension of other spaces shaped by patriarchy and heteronormativity. Our struggle for a feminist Internet is one that forms part of a continuum of our resistance in other spaces, public, private, and in-between.

5. Movement building
The internet is a transformative political space. It facilitates new forms of citizenship that enable individuals to claim, construct and express selves, genders, and sexualities. This includes connecting across territories, demanding accountability and transparency, and creating opportunities for sustained feminist movement building.

6. Decision making in Internet governance

We believe in challenging the patriarchal spaces and processes that control internet governance, as well as having more feminists and queers at the decision-making tables. We want to democratize policy making affecting the internet, as well as diffuse ownership of and power in global and local networks.

Economy

7. Alternative economies

We are committed to interrogating the capitalist logic that drives technology towards further privatization, profit, and corporate control. We work to create alternative forms of economic power that are grounded in principles of cooperation, solidarity, commons, environmental sustainability, and openness.

8. Free and open source

We are committed to creating and experimenting with technology, including digital safety and security, and using free/libre and open source software (FLOSS), tools, and platforms. Promoting, disseminating, and sharing knowledge about the use of FLOSS is central to our praxis.

Expression

9. Amplifying feminist discourse

We claim the power of the internet to amplify women's narratives and lived realities. There is a need to resist the state, the religious right and other extremist forces that monopolize discourses of morality, while silencing feminist voices and persecuting women's human rights defenders.

10. Freedom of expression

We defend the right to sexual expression as a freedom of expression issue of no less importance than political or religious expression. We strongly object to the efforts of state and non-state actors to control, surveil, regulate, and restrict feminist and queer expression on the internet through technology, legislation, or violence. We recognize this as part of the larger political project of moral policing, censorship, and hierarchization of citizenship and rights.

11. Pornography and "harmful content"

We recognize that the issue of online pornography has to do with agency, consent, power, and labor. We reject simple causal linkages made between consumption of pornographic content and violence against women. We also reject the use of the umbrella term "harmful content" to label expression on female and transgender sexuality. We support reclaiming and creating alternative erotic content that resists the mainstream patriarchal gaze and locates women and queer persons' desires at the center.

Agency

12. Consent

We call for the need to build an ethics and politics of consent into the culture, design, policies, and terms of service of online platforms. Women's agency lies in their ability to make informed decisions on what aspects of their public or private lives to share online.

13. Privacy and data

We support the right to privacy and to full control over personal data and information online at all levels. We reject the practices of states and private companies that use data for profit and to manipulate online behavior. Surveillance is the historical tool of patriarchy, used to control and restrict women's bodies, speech, and activism. We pay equal attention to surveillance practices of individuals, the private sector, as well as state and non-state actors.

14. Memory

We have the right to exercise and retain control over our personal history and memory on the internet. This includes being able to access all our personal data and information online, and to be able to exercise control over this data, including knowing who has access to it and under what conditions, and the ability to delete it forever.

15. Anonymity

We defend the right to be anonymous and reject all claims to restrict anonymity online. Anonymity enables our freedom of expression online, particularly when it comes to breaking taboos of sexuality and heteronormativity, experimenting with gender identity, and enabling safety for women and queer persons affected by discrimination.

16. Children and youth

We call for the inclusion of the voices and experiences of young people in the decisions made about safety and security online and promote their safety, privacy, and access to information. We recognize children's right to healthy emotional and sexual development, which includes the right to privacy and access to positive information about sex, gender, and sexuality at critical times in their lives.

17. Online violence

We call on all internet stakeholders, including internet users, policy makers, and the private sector to address the issue of online harassment and technology-related violence. The attacks, threats, intimidation, and policing experienced by women and queer persons are real, harmful and alarming, and are part of the broader issue of gender-based violence. It is our collective responsibility to address and end this.

VIRAL PERFORMANCES OF GENDER

Christina Grammatikopoulou

OVER THE PAST DECADE FEMINISM HAS BECOME A UBIQUITOUS TERM, appearing in debates regarding gender equality, sexism entrenched in everyday culture, and the right to make choices for one's own body but also as a glittery brand used to promote products and services. Whether this popularization of a radical activist movement has led to an advancement of its causes is yet to be evaluated. However, we can begin to understand feminism's impact by considering its manifestations in politics and visual culture that have been put into the spotlight during the last 10 years. In this essay, I discuss the work of artists who express feminist issues, focusing on how they use "virality" and "noise" as communicative strategies. In order to put their work into context, I examine how, through its new strategies, feminism gains ground within connected and disconnected spaces, but also how the same strategies can be turned against it – be it through open attacks against feminist manifestations or the abusive appropriation of the term feminism. In any case, the artists presented below seem to be aware of the contradictions emerging in the conflict area between activism, trolling and marketing, and use exactly these contradictions as an integral part of their work.

The selection criteria of the material are both generational – focusing on "digital natives," who were brought up after the expansion of the Internet – and thematic, i.e. choosing works that deal with topics central to contemporary feminism, such as sexual assault, body positivity – the idea that all bodies are beautiful, regardless of age, shape and race – and gender stereotypes. The sources come mainly from online articles that deal with the separate issues discussed here – regarding feminism and troll culture – as there have been very few academic studies of these phenomena to this date.

The inherent difficulty of defining and criticizing such artworks and actions is embraced as being representative of the argument of communicative "noise" that is central to this text. Noise, in this context, defines the interception and confusion introduced deliberately across communication platforms in order to make a message less clear to its recipients. Such noise can be the result of the nature of online platforms, where constant content updates are essential and new information needs to be added, regardless of its accuracy or relevance. Often enough, there is deliberation behind it, as fake news is presented alongside facts and ideas that are met with trolling.

Central to the approach of this text is to understand the "Expanded Space" as a novel space that defines the consequences and reception of the artworks. The everyday experience of most people now takes place within this continuum of online and offline spaces, whereby the digital networked space, experienced through the permanent use of computers and mobile communication tools, constantly transforms the experience of physical space. The understanding of space that goes along with this implies not starting from two separate poles of connectivity, not thinking in categories of online and offline, but understanding space as a sum of all possibilities: physical, expanded, virtual, mixed, and hybrid. The latest buzzword for this understanding of space, most often seen in business and marketing, is "phygital." For the purpose of this essay I choose, however, to employ the rather descriptive term "Expanded Space" is preferred. I intend to emphasize the openness and the development potential of this space and to express the fusion of the physical and the digital driven by new technologies. As the artists and activists integral to the argument made in this text are too young to remember a pre-internet world, it would be natural to assume that, for them, the continuity of these spaces is a given, especially compared to the previous generations, for whom connectivity gradually came to form part of their everyday experience. Below, I refer to contemporary feminism and feminist art, which preferably materialize in this Expanded Space where both connected and disconnected experiences intersect and mutually influence each other.

Borrowed from biology, the term "virality" refers in media culture to the communication of any idea, image, video, or meme to which numerous users react. A viral post is shared horizontally – i.e. it is not sent directly from a source to a large number of users but rather from a source to users who then re-share it millions of times, thus allowing the post to reach a far greater number of people. It is also important to emphasize that virality is generated by the audience, and this means that as many people as possible must find the "story" interesting if they are to share it. For this reason, different types of tricks are often employed to generate virality: News stories are presented in an exaggerated way, include visually well-staged protests, or humorous memes. In other words, virality can serve a variety of purposes, from raising awareness to trolling or click baiting. It can express and reproduce existing power structures, but also transforms them in unexpected ways.

One of the biggest challenges in dealing with the wide spectrum of contemporary feminism is to understand its true dimensions and to evaluate the significance and interdependencies of its various manifestations. In this regard, it could be helpful to begin on a small scale before proceeding towards larger contexts and concepts. Accordingly, my essay begins with artistic works in which themes and contradictions characteristic of contemporary feminism are expressed in different ways. A more comprehensive overview of the conditions, forms of expression, and potentials of contemporary feminism will then be developed, illustrating the connection between online and offline protests. Finally, the focus will be shifted towards how viral tactics are used by marketing experts and anti-feminists – in similar ways, but each for very different purposes – thus generating noise that is often heard louder than feminist voices.

Feminist Performances of Gender

Contemporary feminist artists are performing within a space where women's bodies become subject to presentation, optimization, monetization, criticism, and even attacks. It is a space extended by digital networked technologies where the potential to be seen and to interact with the audience is significantly amplified. The works often enter into dialogue with art history or reflect aspects of digital culture. More specifically, they question the traditional images of women, created by and for the male gaze, as they adhere to or subvert the poses and expressions of women that are widespread throughout art history and the media. The feminist performance artists examined here have control over how they present themselves to the gaze of others. They are both subjects and objects of their work, and manifest both their interiors – experience and knowledge, and their exteriors – bodily and aesthetic forms. The reception of their works reflects the duality of the artist as simultaneously the object and subject of representation: In endless commentaries, the appearance of both the work and the artists are the objects of criticism and praise,

One of the best-known artworks that emerged as an act of protest is *Carry That Weight* (2014/15) by Emma Sulkowicz. The endurance performance denounced the rape of the artist by one of her fellow students during her studies at Columbia University and the subsequent dismissal of the case by the authorities. For nine months prior to graduation – the average length of a pregnancy – the performer carried a mattress around Campus, mostly alone, unless someone offered to help. Thus, Sulkowicz brought a personal experience, which was to be concealed, into the public space and symbolically showed her burden through the real weight of the mattress. The work quickly aroused great media interest, especially online, where it was received in an extremely polarized way: *Artnet*, the *New York Times*, and various feminist platforms praised it as one of the most important works of art of the year, while critics accused it of victimizing women. As the performance went viral, media attention shifted from the artwork to the story behind it. In social media, the work and the artist became the subject of violent attacks: Men's rights activists launched a smear campaign against the artist, while the alleged rapist accused Sulkowicz of harassment.

The memory of the rape is re-enacted by the artist in *Ceci n'est pas un viol* (2015), an online performance that consists of a video, an introductory text by the artist, and a comments section. In contrast to the symbolic character of the *Mattress Performance*, here we have a representation of the events that traumatized the artist depicted on film, in a quality resembling the aesthetics of surveillance camera footage. This puts the viewers in the position of a police officer or a jury member examining the evidence before they make up their mind about what might have happened that day – a position that many social media users assumed anyway once the story went viral. The online space of the performance was open to trolls enraged about the first performance, giving them the opportunity to consume the image of the artist's body and post hateful remarks. In fact, the comments were an intended part of the performance. They show how rape victims who talk about their traumatic experiences are subjected to further humiliation. Without the artist's initial questions regarding the work and the visitors' comments, it would be easy to confuse the video with any online pornographic material. Providing only a few initial questions, the artist maintains a distanced approach throughout the performance, further highlighting the rage of her critics.

This puts into perspective the artist Ann Hirsch's statement that "[…] whenever you put your body online, in some way you are in conversation with porn." Hirsch's *Playground* (2013) also plays with sexuality and memory, but her work is even more nuanced. The live performance is set in the late 1990s, in a fictitious chat room in which two protagonists, a 12-year-old girl and a 27-year-old man, meet and "fall in love." The work is based on the artist's real experience of an online relationship with a much older man when she was in her early teens. For her even then, when the distinction between "real life" and "digital life" was much clearer, virtual communication felt very real. However, as the conversation evolves from a casual encounter to ever more intimate confessions, one could ask whether the emerging emotions reflect the course of the relationship or, rather, arise primarily from the artist's imagination. Now an adult, the artist reflects on her past, alternating between her lived experience and the classification of that experience from today's perspective. The result is a critical view of a relationship with unequal dynamics, in which the sexual awakening of the teenager involved with an older man is presented as problematic.

Hirsch is particularly interested in online popular culture and the ways in which women might inhabit it. In her *Scandalishious* project (2008), she presented herself as "Caroline," a "hipster college freshman" that published videos of herself dancing, reciting poems, and divulging personal thoughts on her YouTube channel. In this project, the artist tries to combine the two most ubiquitous clichés found on the Internet: A woman who dances in front of the camera and shows her sexuality, and a woman who simply speaks to the camera – and thus to the audience – without any sexual connotations. Thus, Hirsch alludes to the ancient stereotype of women being seen as either sinners or saints. "Caroline" became a huge success with online audiences who were unaware that the videos were in fact an online performance, and thus perceived her just as any other YouTuber, lefet comments, and responded to her videos. By adopting such a volatile character, Hirsch explored hidden sides of her personality and connected with people who reacted to her performance in a multidimensional way.

Amalia Ulman is another artist who slips into different roles and integrates them cleverly into her social media stream, leaving the impression that they are in fact her own personal development. The performance *Excellences & Perfections* (2014) unfolded over four months on her Instagram account. She began publishing images of herself as an attractive girl who has just moved to L.A. and dreams of becoming famous. Her photos were the embodiment of what is commonly understood as "cute": pastel colors, perfectly styled food, and stuffed animals. Soon, she became overly sexualized as a "sugar-babe" that underwent breast-enlargement surgery, attended pole-dancing classes, and lived a lavish lifestyle paid for by her "sugar daddies." Then it was time for redemption, and Ulman's persona was reborn as a "wellness goddess." As she was changing her identity, her followers' comments were changing, too: Critics warned her that she would not be taken seriously in the art world if she was showing off her body on social media, while others congratulated her on her transformation. Eventually, she posted a final picture of a rose, with the caption: "The End."

The reception of Ulman's performance shows that a woman flaunting her own image is always perceived as narcissistic, but she is sometimes forgiven if she does it for a greater good – in this case, for the sake of art. Once it became clear that the post were all part of a performance, the work was shown at renowned art venues (Tate Modern, Whitechapel Art Gallery) and received enthusiastic reviews.

By switching between three personality types in such a short time, Ulman not only irritated her followers, but also emphasized the influence and mechanisms of social media; at the same time, the invented personas gave her the opportunity to experience new situations. Among others, the work raises the question of how "social media influencers" become popular and how they display their lives alongside sponsored content and products. These online celebrities often take on different personae to address specific topics and target groups such as vegan food, fitness, fashion, lifestyle – maximizing their reach and number of "likes." They produce carefully curated images of perfection, unattainable beauty, and lifestyle. In this sense, Ulman's perfectly selected and manipulated Instagram photos, made to look as something that they are not, are not much different from any other social media profile that is created to gain maximum amount of popularity and become commercially successful.

Online popularity is also the focus of Nuria Guiu's interest. Combining her dual capacity as a performer and an anthropology researcher, she presents an interesting discourse regarding the power of "likes." After researching the topic of body language on the Internet, she selected the movements that gathered the most "likes" on YouTube – from pop music to yoga – for her dance performance *Likes* (2018), and used them as elements of her own choreography. The performance evolves slowly, alternating between dance and pauses to communicate with the audience, in order to explain where her movements come from and what they mean. But as the rhythm rapidly intensifies, the dancer performs the fragmented movements almost breathlessly, and without speaking gradually unites them into a raging motion sequence; she sweats and fights until she finally discards her clothes and reveals her body. Guiu's performance shows how social media visibility is linked to prestige and economic power, and what efforts are required to maintain the necessary pace. The performance ends with the image of naked female body. It is also one that is most frequently clicked on, increasing the number of "views" and the related income. At the same time, such image attracts the largest numbers hateful comments due to its strong sexual connotations.

For the Danish artist Maja Malou Lyse, who posts sex-positive self-portraits on her Instagram page, the female body is the starting point of her artistic work – both as image and embodied experience. However, while advocating body positivity, she admits in the captions that she also tends to select the images where she looks slimmer, recognizing the impact of beauty standards on women. At first glance, her Instagram posts are not much different from other pretty Instagrammers that post selfies, apart from the fact that they are accompanied by politically charged comments against rape culture and capitalism. Apart from that, the artist's aesthetics are very close to those of the porn industry: voluptuous looks, sexy underwear, sex toys, and revealing poses. However, she subverts the viewer's expectations by showing aspects of the female body that the male gaze prefers to ignore, such as body hair, menstruation, live streaming of her cervix, and DIY gynecology objects.

The latter is also the focus of Lyse's project *How to Stay out of the Gynecologist's Office* (2016), which revives the self-help gynecology ideas of 1970s feminist groups. In a series of workshops, the artist and the participants share their bodily experiences and exchange knowledge through talking and self-examination. On her Instagram, Lyse provides a starter kit for gynecological self-examination and encourages women to explore their own vaginas. This process of self-discovery should intensify the bodily experience and promote autonomy through newly acquired self-knowledge. At the same time, Lyse addresses the power relations inherent in the patient-doctor relationship – where the patient is often viewed in a fragmented and objectified way.

The artists discussed above reflect on a variety of topics that relate to experiences of women in the Expanded Space. They are not afraid to use stereotypes of femininity in their aesthetics – from beautiful poses to pink colors – in order to make a comment on the image of women in the media. Admittedly, they all belong to a limited demographic group – they are all young, beautiful in the traditional sense, white and cis-gender (with the exception of Sulkowicz, who is of multi-ethnic descent and identifies as non-binary). And yet, their works, and the ways in which they are received, reflect a broad feminist struggle combining elements of protest and performance.

Feminism in the Expanded Space of Digital Networks:
A Fourth Wave?

Feminism is often seen as progressing in waves – something that can be traced back to 1960s journalism. It is true that this vision implies fragmentation, which does not reflect the fact that feminism is a movement with a unique goal – gender equality – that it aims to work through different strategies relating to the needs of different social groups and eras. However, adopting this traditional division can be helpful for making comparisons and that is why I will partially apply it here.

Each wave of feminism has focused on different facets of gender equality: the right to vote and education; inequalities in the workplace and reproductive rights; intersectionality and fight against sexual assault. In this sense, what has been characterized as the "fourth-wave feminism" could be seen as an evolution of the third-wave that challenged misogynist rhetoric in the media and popular culture, while addressing diverse experiences of being a woman – in terms of class, origin, and sexual identity (the word "woman" is used in this text to define anyone that identifies as one, similarly to the references to the "female body.") Fourth-wave feminism recognizes that multiple layers of oppression may coexist, meaning that a middle-class cisgender woman faces different challenges than a POC refugee or a transgender woman. While the first and second waves largely addressed issues relevant to middle and upper class white women, the struggle is now "glocal," i.e. in different dimensions, from local to global, and can relate to universal, as well as very specific problems. However, there are also conflicting issues that stem from the feminists' differing political approaches: There are activists who follow a solidarity and anti-capitalist stance that favors a collective fight against inequalities and take aim against the political systems breeding these inequalities. On the other hand, there's an individualist and liberal-capitalist viewpoint that mainly aims towards breaking the glass ceiling and putting more women in places of political and economic power. What differentiates the fourth-wave from the previous ones, however, is not its focus but its medium.

Like a magnifying glass, the internet has highlighted existing inequalities and multiplied the battlegrounds for equal rights. In the early days, the internet was heralded as a non-hierarchical, democratic space where people would be able to define their life conditions and identity, liberated from the existing restrictions based on race, gender, and the phenomena of social exclusion. Driven by this vision, and understanding the rising significance of communication technology, the Cyberfeminists of the early 1990s such as *VNS Matrix* sought to enhance women's relationship with technology – they believed in its inherent transformative power. However, this techno-determinism did not persist. It soon became clear that social and ideological constructs are entrenched in technology. By the late 1990s, Cyberfeminists such as the *Old Boys Network* moved towards more comprehensive understandings of technology by seeking multiple perspectives and approaches. Looking at OBN closely, we can distinguish two paths that have become significant for contemporary feminism: First, the rejection in their manifesto of generalizing "theses" in favor of "antitheses" – in other words, rather than defining what Cyberfeminism is, they say what it is not, thus leaving room for a variety of approaches. Second and most important, they created a "network," which was active both online and offline in workshops, meetings, conferences, chat rooms, and mailing lists. They explored the potential of getting organized in a "phygital" world that was just beginning to expand. Meanwhile, this expanded space has become the natural place for communities to emerge and feminist campaigns to take place; the place where women meet, learn, discuss, and forge action plans. As studies of some recent feminist protests have shown, the continuity of networked and offline spaces offers entirely new ways of unfolding political forms of action, such as taking virality out onto the streets as a tactical means.

The protests carried out by *Femen* since 2008, usually against specific targets like Vladimir Putin or Silvio Berlusconi, gathered a lot of media attention, not so much thanks to their anti-patriarchy slogans, but rather because the protesters were topless. These actions have stirred great controversy in the feminist world, especially when it was revealed in the media that, initially a man, Victor Svyatski, led the planning and organization of the group. He allegedly selected the women for protests based on whether they met conventional beauty standards and then taught them how they should act. Even though Svyatski had left the group by the time *Femen* went international, the aesthetics of their protests still follow the same performative path: flashing signs written on the chests of young, white, thin, able-bodied women. The protesters are usually held back by police officers within moments of their appearance; however, their topless images live for much longer as they are widely shared online, thus transferring the discourse from the streets to online media. In this sense, the performativity of the protest only makes sense if we view it within the continuous online/offline space as an event that lasts for a few moments offline and lives on online. Even though *Femen's* tactics of virality have brought attention to cases of patriarchal oppression, they have also alienated other feminists, as their stance obviously serves the objectifying male gaze.

Similar controversies surround *Slutwalks*, during which protesters dress as what would be considered a "slut" according to patriarchal logic. The first *Slutwalks* were organized in Toronto in 2011 as a protest against a police officer's remarks that "women should avoid dressing like sluts in order not to become victims." By adopting a derogatory term that stems from "rape culture," the participants sought to undermine the latter, arguing that sexual assault is never the victim's fault. Even though not all protesters opt for "slutty" clothes, the images appearing on social media are usually of beautiful women exposing their bodies. Once more, the discourse centers on the objectification of women and the tendency to conform to standards set by the beauty or porn industries. As was the case with the artists discussed above, the women who decide to reveal their bodies act both as the subject of action and scrutiny.

Different groups of women and gender activists have different priorities, so it is not surprising that the "fourth wave" appears fragmented in relation to both its concerns and scope. It is undisputed, however, that these fragments add up a growing wave that has attracted media attention and fueled political discourse, especially over the last two years.

The Women's March (2017), which took place in different cities across the United States, was accompanied by many smaller solidarity protests worldwide. With a total of more than five million demonstrators, it set a new record in the history of the United States for a one-day protest. The demonstrations were triggered by the inauguration of Donald Trump as President of the United States. In the past, Trump has demonstrated a disparaging attitude towards women and announced changes to the abortion laws. One should note here the presence of hashtags (common since the 2011 Occupy Movement) on protest signs. The hashtags reflect the continuity of online and offline space and the presumption that the images of the protesters will be shared on social media. The protesters' pink knitted hats with pointed tips resembling cat ears – the "pussy hats" – were a reference to Trump's comments that "he grabs women by the pussy." The hats gave a pink tone to the images of the protests. Rather than rejecting the stereotypical color and "girly" aesthetics, most contemporary feminists embraced it.

In the same year, another record-breaking protest took place, this time primarily online. The *#MeToo* campaign was launched in 2006 by Tarana Burke, a black activist, as a way to show empathy to young victims of sexual abuse. The slogan didn't go viral until 2017, when actor Alyssa Milano suggested that everyone affected by sexual harassment or sexual assault should use the hashtag *#MeToo* to share their experiences. Within a day, the hashtag was used over 500,000 times on Twitter and 4.7 million times on Facebook. The online campaign meant real-life repercussions for some of the perpetrators of the offences, such as the film producer Harvey Weinstein, who had to say goodbye to his powerful position and is now being prosecuted. At the same time, the campaign as beneficial to some of the victims, who felt empowered by the discussion to speak out against the injustices they have faced.

Last but not least, the dynamics of the *#MeToo* movement have contributed to massive turnout in subsequent feminist protests worldwide. On March 8 2018, women in Spain called for a strike for equal rights at work and demanded an end to domestic violence, femicide, and sexual assault. On the eve of the march, a nocturnal gathering was held demanding the right to take to the streets without fear of assault. The atmosphere was particularly charged in light of recent rapes reported in the news, such as the "Wolfpack" trial that would, again, spark large-scale nationwide protests two months later following the apparently unfair ruling. The International Women's Day strike saw hundreds of thousands taking to the streets and over 5.3 million workers skipping work. It was a strike on an unprecedented scale. The main slogan, "Si paramos el mundo para" ["When we stop, the world stops"], showed the determination of the protesters and the sheer number of people on the streets – all traffic had to be stopped. Social media feeds not only represented the events, but also showed that the flood of news contributed to the scale of mobilization. Comparing this massive protest with the Spanish solidarity protest for the American Women's March, which brought together only a handful of people, one could conclude that the Women's Day demonstration in Spain was successful because it addressed concrete problems faced by women from all walks of life in Spain. The massive scale of the protests, therefore, suggests that it is not enough to have a universal vision to mobilize the masses; rather, a specific local agenda that would unite different groups in the fight against particular problems.

Viral Noise
From Trolls to Influencers

A recurring pattern in the development of digital technology seems to be, at the beginning, the inflated optimism. Just as in the early days of the internet, a new hope arose in the years after 2005: The public's active participation in publishing content would lead to the development of independent news sites and thus to better quality of news, freed from corporate control. The emergence of social media and the attendant opportunities for groups to communicate promptly and cheaply, exchange information, and organize autonomously made this perspective even more realistic. In 2011, when the Arab Spring and the Occupy movement spread worldwide, blogs and social media were often viewed as "spaces of democracy," while trolls and hackers were seen as heroic figures enabling progressive activism through *détournement* – employing the tools of the system against the system itself.

However, the same tools and methods are now used by groups that want to influence a broad audience – but with a different objective. From troll factories, fake news sites, online vigilantes, and hackers to government agencies and intelligence services, everyone today uses the same means to manipulate: to influence election results, harass marginalized groups, manipulate facts, or simply sell products. To name all these phenomena in one breath does not mean that they are all the same. It is merely intended to illustrate that various groups use virality as a tactic – just as feminists do. And while the feminist movement is gaining momentum worldwide thanks to new communication strategies, the Men's Rights Activists (MRAs) and other radical groups of the extreme right are also gaining influence through the use of the same strategies.

The economic crisis of the last decade has prepared the ground for radical extremists, who are responsible for violent actions – from Athens to Charlottesville. What is significant to stress is that the extreme right neophytes are often radicalized through online platforms, where they also coordinate their efforts against their targets, such as ethnic minorities, migrants, or feminists. This type of behavior has become so commonplace that even in online discussions about games, sports, or politics, women who dare to express their opinion are met with hostility.

The seemingly harmless "mansplaining" belongs to the scale of discriminatory forms of behavior. Although the phenomenon is hardly new, social media have contributed significantly to its spread as public contributions can be commented on by anyone. Another tactic is attacking a straw man, the deliberate attempt to create a confrontation in which the other's arguments are twisted to make them sound absurd. The most common tactic, however, is less subtle: online disputes often escalate very quickly to rape and murder threats, even within communities that are considered progressive. The increased aggressiveness is blamed on online anonymity, which combined with troll culture promoted across popular forums, is blossoming. Users of 4chan, for example, repeatedly try to deceive mainstream media with absurd information – just for "fun." Even though 4chan's cultural influence is often exaggerated, these viral tactics have contributed significantly to the formation of troll armies that spread fake news in the US in the wake of the 2016 election and repeatedly launched smear campaigns against individuals.

Gamergate is one of the best-known examples of how the culture of abuse is turned against women who dare to enter what is considered to be a male-dominated space. It started with an orchestrated attack against Zoe Quinn, a successful game developer, after her ex-boyfriend claimed that she had cheated on him in 2014. Alleged cheating is a useful tool for internet "vigilantes" who feel that the woman needs to be punished for her actions; it is the most frequently used claim in revenge porn websites, where intimate photos and videos of women are shared alongside their names, telephone numbers, and address details by vindictive ex-partners. Quinn's haters, who had often spoken against her about what they felt was an undeserved success, were finally given a "reason" to feel righteous in their attacks. This hate campaign against a woman linked to the gaming community was not the first and would certainly not be the last: Two years earlier, Anita Sarkeesian received similar treatment for her YouTube series "Tropes vs. Women in Video Games," as did tech culture journalist Leigh Alexander, actress and professional gamer Felicia Day, and developer Brianna Wu. The public threats of murder and rape and the disclosure of private contact information had a real impact on the victims, who had to withdraw from their environment and sometimes even give up their homes in order to escape the attacks. When Quinn sought justice, the judge advised her to "go offline," much like women are advised to stay out of public space to be safe.

Gamergate revealed how a troll army can gain power. This included spreading untrue stories by cleverly manipulating search engines and social media algorithms with tags and meta-data that made their stories appear at the top of Twitter, Facebook, or Google searches. The manipulation of facts by right wing and reactionary groups reveals a solid knowledge of online media, and their actions show how virality and noise help to stifle real news in the flood of information or silence women with confusion, fake news, and hate campaigns.

One of the extremist "stars" that emerged from the scandal was Milo Yiannopoulos, who was covering the story for Breitbart, a conservative news site that became instrumental in the making and spreading of fake news, especially before the last US election. Yiannopoulos' texts and speeches are representative of the tactics of noise: A gay man himself married to a black man, he speaks against gay culture and non-white people; he often makes outrageous claims and when they backfire, he says that it was just satire – for example, claiming that he's happy about the deaths of Syrian children or that it is acceptable to harass 13-year-old boys. He usually masks his offensive behavior as "opinion" and the harassment of others as defense of "free speech." "Satire" and "humor" are also often used as arguments in anti-women online campaigns: "Doing it for the lulz" is the insider term for it, which means doing something for fun. The expression comes from 4chan's environment and has always ignored the real injuries caused by this kind of assault.

The language of online trolls and anti-feminists has become particularly popular with right-wing populists and has received a new boost since Donald Trump came into power. They like to use vague source attribution (such as "everyone knows that"), personal affirmation (such as "trust me"), exaggerated adjectives (such as "the most fantastic," "absolutely most horrible"), personal stories as solid arguments, and above all – sentences that are never finished in the verbose form of repetition and paraphrase and are therefore confusing for the audience. The term "Trump-speak" refers to this kind of populist speech that aims to generate impact, rather than communicate an idea, while it dismisses eloquence as "elitist." Spending a few minutes on the YouTube channels of Alt-right and Men's Rights Activists (MRAs), these language patterns quickly become apparent. As examples, the videos "Why modern women are unhappy" (by Milo Yiannopoulos) or "Why are women being educated" (Roosh V) can be considered; in the latter the portrait of the 45th President of the USA hangs in the background.

The "problem" being discussed in the above videos is feminism, which allegedly discourages women from fulfilling their purpose in life. But women are not the only ones to suffer from feminism: According to the men's rights groups, feminism is responsible for the decline of Western civilization as a whole, forcing men to become "female" or "beta" in order to find a partner at all. To counter this problem, the MRAs give advice on how to restore and maintain masculinity. Pick Up Artists (PUAs), for example, focus on the "game" or, as they vividly describe it, "fucking" as many women as possible. The members of the Men Going Their Own Way group, on the other hand, opt for celibacy as a consequence of their contempt for women who are sexually liberated and manipulative (supposedly just trying to lure them into marriage), and therefore are too dirty for them. Involuntary Celibates (Incels), on the other hand, consider women too powerful because of their ability to choose; women would prefer better-looking men and thus have control over the sexual fulfillment of men. The Incels are looking forward to a rebellion against this *status quo* and the fact that beta men will also get their chance. In the meantime, their rage had deadly consequences on several occasions: the massive shooting in Santa Barbara (2014) by Roger Elliot and the van attack in Toronto (2018) by Alek Minassian – both of whom declared their allegiance to the Incel movement before the attacks and blamed "women" for being the cause of their actions because they refuse to have sex with them.

Female agency in sex is the big issue for these men, who insult feminists online for being "sluts," "too promiscuous," or for making themselves undesirable for men. Even if it is not a question of a woman acting in a male space – as in *Gamergate* – or actively campaigning for women's rights, she can still anger the trolls if she reveals herself as an "attention whore." For many trolls, feminist artists mentioned earlier, who question gender stereotypes by making them visible in an exaggerated way and claim the male territory for self-determined display of female bodies, certainly belong to this group.

Whereas in the case of trolls and men's rights activists you can easily unveil their tactics of noise, it might not be so straightforward to draw the line in actions that claim to be "empowering" for women. Nevertheless, it is important, as we examine the space where contemporary feminism takes place, to say – in accordance with the Old Boys Network antitheses manifesto – what contemporary feminism is *not*. Today, anything a woman does can be portrayed as empowering: Indulging in consumption, publishing images of her body as a sign of self-confidence and body positivity, wearing a T-shirt with the word "feminist" on it, although it may have been sewn by a woman in a third world country who does not even receive the minimum wage for her work. In addition, social media influencers and digital marketing strategists are appropriating the increasingly popular feminism to further establish their products and brands with its help. Using the term feminism for purposes that have nothing to do with social and political activism weakens its potential in the struggle against gender inequality and instead associates it with consumer culture, the objectification of one's own image and the exploitation of unjustly paid labor.

Notably, these claims of "empowerment" are being replicated in the same online platforms where harassment campaigns against women are being carried out, with technology companies owning these platforms repeatedly failing to protect the victims – because their business model consists in making a profit out of users' data, they do not make an effort to curtail hate speech and fake news that create a hostile environment for women – and other marginalized groups – as it might have an impact on their popularity.

Conclusions

Contemporary feminism is defined by the cross-pollination of digital and physical space, generating new tools of resistance through visual and media culture. The study of various forms of expression of the feminist movement, often referred to as the "fourth wave," reveals several contradictions: Feminism is gaining popularity and retaining much of its militancy – on the street and on the internet – but often manifests itself in affirmative forms; it takes advantage of virality and noise to establish its presence, but the same tactics are also used for harassment campaigns or completely apolitical purposes. Ultimately, viral performances of gender can be attributed not just to activists and artists who advocate feminism but also to the opposite side: The MRAs who want to express an outdated version of masculinity and white male domination. The confusion about the meaning of feminism by people either claiming feminist views under false premises or fighting against it is a sign of our times. Contemporary feminists who do not want to disappear among all the trolls and marketing experts are forced to experiment with new strategies of visibility.

The artists who visualize problems of contemporary feminism seem to be aware of the contradictions and use the same strategies as subjects or tools for their work. Other feminists and anti-feminists often denigrate them as narcissists. This label is often applied to digital natives who grew up with social media and who take it for granted to share their images, preferences, and thoughts with strangers. At the same time, female creators have always been accused of narcissism whenever they abandoned their ancestral function as "neutral objects or surfaces" and instead presented their bodies in a self-determined way. Women are generally regarded as sex objects, as Lucy Lippard notes. This leads to the assumption that every woman who presents her naked body in public only does so because she thinks she is beautiful. The feminist artists presented here do not completely reject common ideals of beauty, such as those found in magazines, porn films, and art history; they understand their importance, but also try to escape their power of definition and instead allow themselves to play with them. Their eclectic aesthetics therefore often consist of different sources and refer to very different aesthetics. Men often feel excluded by this kind of self-portrayal of women, especially when the images break with traditional notions of female attractiveness.

So where do feminist artists of the digital age draw the line between feminism and consumer culture, between feminist activism and noise? Instead of drawing such a line, they intentionally blur it, using their performances to question the limits between staged performance and reality, empowerment and objectification. The border is marked by its blurring.

Bibliography

Bennett Catherine, "Violent misogyny is unfortunately not confined to the internet's 'incels'," *The Guardian*. Available online: https://www.theguardian.com/commentisfree/2018/apr/29/violent-misogyny-not-confined-to-internet-incels

Brockes, Emma, "Me Too founder Tarana Burke: 'You have to use your privilege to serve other people'," *The Guardian*. Available online: https://www.theguardian.com/world/2018/jan/15/me-too-founder-tarana-burke-women-sexual-assault

Broomfield, Matt. "Women's March against Donald Trump is the largest day of protests in US history, say political scientists." *Independent*. Available online: https://www.independent.co.uk/news/world/americas/womens-march-anti-donald-trump-womens-rights-largest-protest-demonstration-us-history-political-a7541081.html

Burke, Sarah, "Crying on Camera: "fourth-wave feminism" and the threat of commodification." Available online: https://openspace.sfmoma.org/2016/05/crying-on-camera-fourth-wave-feminism-and-the-threat-of-commodification/

Carole Cadwalladr, "Google is not 'just' a platform. It frames, shapes and distorts how we see the world," *The Guardian*. Available online: https://www.theguardian.com/commentisfree/2016/dec/11/google-frames-shapes-and-distorts-how-we-see-world

Davis, Ben, "Columbia Student's Striking Mattress Performance," *Artnet*. Available online: https://news.artnet.com/opinion/columbia-students-striking-mattress-performance-92346

Guiu, Núria, "Likes I. Body Language on the Internet." Available online: http://www.nuriaguiu.com/antropology/2017/1/3/14m8awkm9gkop68pifsetnbdvdmaeo

Guiu, Núria, "Likes II. Numbers and Capital." Available online: http://www.nuriaguiu.com/antropology/2017/7/3/d9qqo1kjof5vc5zujbb4mbfy105apz

Jones, Amelia, *Body Art/ Performing the Subject*, Minneapolis/London: University of Minnesota Press, 1998.

Jones, Sam, "More than 5m join Spain's 'feminist strike,' unions say," *The Guardian*, Available online: https://www.theguardian.com/world/2018/mar/08/spanish-women-give-up-work-for-a-day-in-first-feminist-strike

Jones, Sam, "Protests in Spain as five men cleared of teenager's gang rape," *The Guardian*, Available online: https://www.theguardian.com/world/2018/apr/26/protests-spain-five-men-cleared-of-teenagers-gang-rape-pamplona

Lippard, Lucy, "The Pains and Pleasures of Rebirth: European and American Women's Body Art," *Art In America*, 64 (3) (1976): 73-81.f

Locke, Abigail; Lauthom, Rebecca; Lyons, Antonia, "Social media platforms as complex and contradictory spaces for feminisms: Visibility, opportunity, power, resistance and activism," *Feminism & Psychology,* 2088, Vol.28(1) 3-10.

Malone, Noreen, "Zoë and the Trolls. Video-game designer Zoë Quinn survived Gamergate, an act of web harassment with world-altering implications," *Select/All,* Available online: http://nymag.com/selectall/2017/07/zoe-quinn-surviving-gamergate.html

Muntro, Ealasaid, "Feminism: A fourth wave?," Available online: https://www.psa.ac.uk/insight-plus/feminism-fourth-wave

Nagle, Angela, *Kill All Normies. Online Culture Wars from 4chan and Tumblr to Trump and the Alt-Right,* Winchester / Washington: Zero Books, 2017.

Nahon, Karine; Hemsley, Jeff, *Going Viral,* Malden: Polity Press, 2013.

Old Boys Network, "100 anti-theses." Available online: https://www.obn.org/reading_room/fs_read.html

Ruigrok, Sophie, "How this 2014 Instagram hoax predicted the way we now use social media," *Dazed,* Available online: http://www.dazeddigital.com/art-photography/article/39375/1/amalia-ulman-2014-instagram-hoax-predicted-the-way-we-use-social-media

Smith-Prei, Carrie; Stehle, Maria, *Awkward Politics: Technologies of Popfeminist Activism,* Montreal & Kingston / London / Chicago: McGill-Queen's University Press, 2016.

Smith, Roberta, "In a Mattress, a Level for Art and Political Protest," *The New York Times,* Available online: https://www.nytimes.com/2014/09/22/arts/design/in-a-mattress-a-fulcrum-of-art-and-political-protest.html

Sollfrank, Cornelia, "Revisiting the Future. Cornelia Sollfrank on Cyberfeminism Then and Now." Available online: https://transmediale.de/content/revisiting-the-future

Tynan, Dan, "Revenge porn: the industry profiting from online abuse," *The Guardian,* Available online: https://www.theguardian.com/technology/2016/apr/26/revenge-porn-nude-photos-online-abuse

Valenti, Jessica, "SlutWalks and the future of feminism," *The Washington Post.* Available online: https://www.washingtonpost.com/opinions/slutwalks-and-the-future-of-feminism/2011/06/01/AGjB9LIH_story.html

Volkart, Yvonne, "Technologies of Identity," in: Marina Grzinic/Adele Eisenstein, (eds.): *The Body Cought in the Intestines of the Computer and Beyond. Women's Strategies and/or Strategies by Women in Media, Art and Theory,* Ljubljana: Maribor, 2000. Available online: http://obn.org/reading_room/writings/html/technologies.html

Weigel, Moira, "Portrait of the Internet as a Young Girl," *Rhizome*. Available online: http://rhizome.org/editorial/2013/sep/30/portrait-internet-young-girl/

Zeisler, Andi, *We Were Feminists Once: From Riot Grrrl to CoverGirl®, the Buying and Selling of a Political Movement*, New York: Public Affairs, 2016.

YouTube:

Daryush Valizadeh, *Roosh V Youtube Channel*, https://www.youtube.com/channel/UC16j6EppP0K85CzYMduNCqw

Milo Yiannopoulos, *MILO Youtube Channel*, https://www.youtube.com/channel/UC0aVoboXBUx2-tVIWHc3W2Q

TECHNO-ECOFEMINISM

Nonhuman Sensations in Technoplanetary Layers

Yvonne Volkart

Translated by Rebecca van Dykes

"The devaluation of care is not very far from
the devaluation of the environment, from
a society that destroys the environment,
from the negation of the body."
– Precarias a la Deriva[1]

THE FEELING THAT THE POSSIBILITIES OF EXISTENCE ON PLANET EARTH
are becoming increasingly limited and allowing less and less scope for
action has become prevalent in recent years. It is necessary to look the

---

1   Precarias a la Deriva, *Globalisierte Sorge*, p. 42.

possible extinction of the human species and many other living things in the eye – not caused by a spectacular war of the worlds, but, much more ordinary, by the way people treat the "environment." "Nature" is striking back. "Gaia" is intruding, is how Isabelle Stengers describes this ontological force, this planetary creature that determines us and is now stalking us with a barbarism that is "blind to the damage she causes, in the manner of everything that intrudes."[2]

How can we live with the contradictory experience that we are part of technocapitalistic acceleration whose playful front and barbarian back oppress us on a daily basis? How can I sense pleasure if my feelings and desires are controlled algorithmically, always longing for more? If the waste my existence produces, instead of disappearing with time, merely disintegrates into even smaller pieces? Waste, about which we do not know what it will do with us. When my eating and travel habits contribute to global warming, which leads to changes in ocean currents, migration, and to the mutation of plants and animals? When we do not know if it will become very cold or very hot? When we have to acknowledge that it was "only" in the last twenty to thirty years that major species extinction began go occur?

I am not only right in the middle of it, in the networked and virtualized era of cyberpunk, which at the time, when we read "Neuromancer" or "He, She and It," I did not imagine to be so ordinary; rather, what is more is that I also belong to that reprehensible species (the "human" species) that takes control of, pollutes, and eradicates everything. But I am also a mother, cyborg, art theorist, bacteria, water, plant, subjectified "in the belly of the monster;"[3] I am a sentient, moving, feeling being, an earthling with and among others. I exist, I am open, I am …

… not accepting the apparently inevitable intensification of extensive forms of exploitation and the paralyses and fears that accompany the discourse on the Anthropocene, which have recently led to a revival of feminist and ecological concerns, not only in art and theory – my area of study – but in everyday practices and activist resistance as well. Concerns regarding the desire for becoming, for relationships and exchange, for coexistence and care, for attention and participation, for

---

2 Isabelle Stengers, *In Catastrophic Times*, p. 43. Stengers's concept of "Gaia" does not correspond to that of deep ecology.

3 Donna Haraway, *The Promises of Monsters*, p. 298.

love and empathy. Concerns, that feminists and ecologists have always considered worthy of investigating and theorizing. Since the eras of hippies and deep ecology, there does not seem to have been any movements in art and theory in which existential needs for commoning and sharing, presence, affect, and immersion with others have been articulated as new values – and this against the background of technological innovation and economic growth, where the values of care and feelings are ridiculed and feminized.

In our Western culture, "women and household (*oikos*)" and "women and nature" are practically synonyms. However, women and technology are also readily equated, in particular when women embody the capitalist machine and its products, such as, for instance, the mechanical women Olimpia in *The Sandman*, Maria in *Metropolis*, or Dolores and Maeve in *Westworld*. Women have examined these equations and reacted differently to them, and hence taken action. For the current text, two apparently diametrical movements are of interest: technofeminism and ecofeminism and their present concurrence that I advocate. Unlike technofeminist approaches, ecofeminism is less widely received and often devalued as essentialist. It has attracted more attention, however, with the renewed interest in feminism and ecology. The most promising developments point to a concurrence of both movements. The corresponding key words are New Materialism, Anthropocene Feminism, and Politics of Care.[4]

The "old" ecofeminist question of how people treat nature, which technologies they explore, and how other relationships can be established with nonhuman beings has become one of the most central questions in the Anthropocene. Inasmuch as technocapitalism always seeks to solve the really big questions by using new technologies whose impact is unknown (geoengineering, electric cars, dissolving plastic waste, et cetera), the "old" cyber- or technofeminist question also has to be asked and reformulated: What role do technologies play in our subjectification? And not just new technologies, but old, for example indigenous, ones as well. This question concerning subjectification/subordination through technologies has to be supplemented by new materialist approaches that inquire into the role technologies play or do not play in the restructuring of our diverse relationships with nonhuman and human beings. It also becomes apparent here that while

---

4   Publications on these are listed in the bibliography.

questions about relationships have hitherto constituted the core area of feminist issues, the achievement of feminism is not acknowledged in the current museum and aesthetic discourse on techno-ecologies and the Anthropocene to the extent it deserves to be.[5]

Referring to selected artistic projects, I attempt to bring together these two apparently diametrically opposed movements – technofeminism and ecofeminism. I assert that the most advanced approaches currently emphasize not only the vitality and transformational power of organisms and matter, but also examine and facilitate relationships between different beings. In other words: If cyberfeminism was concerned with creating feminist, technohybrid concepts of subjects that were fluid, no-longer-only-human, bacterial, female, and queer, and, as its self-proclaimed successor feminism, xenofeminism propagates alienated techno-artifacts, then techno-ecofeminism focuses on the vitality, transformational power, and relationality of human and nonhuman entities and their different temporalities. It is about the *oikos*, the household understood in both a macro- as well as microscopic sense, that is to say, with connections, with couplings and decouplings, sequences and effects. Feminist techno-eco-subjectivity is a vibrant assemblage of concatenations, a relay of pulsating circuits and non/human movements, communication, and sentiments in the technoplanetary layers and deposits called Earth.

As I demonstrate, art succeeds in breaking open the alienation of naturalist ideologemes by means of calculated strategies and the production of an excess of meaning that aesthetically activates the vitality of being-with-others without denying the catastrophic aspect of the Anthropocene.

Scripting the Seascape:
Acoustic Ocean as a Non-Human Radio

The video opens with a shot of an eerily blue landscape, flat-topped mountains with white plateaus and ridged slopes, and is accompanied by a swelling electronic sound punctuated by oddly threatening tones. This uncanny, unfamiliar image is of a 3-D model of the ocean floor and the sounds of communicating fish. The rhythmically fading text

---

5   The symposium "Territories that Matter: Gender, Art and Ecology," Madrid, November 23-24, 2018, sought to address this imbalance.

Fig. 1 (top) and Fig. 2 (below): Video stills from Ursula Biemann: Acoustic Ocean

describes how, in the mid-1940s, a sound channel was discovered in the North Atlantic Ocean. Because of its specific physical nature, the water in the SOFAR (SOund Fixing And Ranging) channel can relay submarine sound waves over several thousand kilometers. It was used in World War II as a "natural" medium for the transmission of distress calls. During the Cold War, hydrophones embedded in it monitored submarine traffic and espionage technologies detected unknown sounds. They could later be decoded as low-frequency waves emitted by blue whales and finback whales – an acoustic ecology that was previously inaudible.

The next shot reveals a pebbled shore and a woman wearing an orange neoprene suit. She unpacks a case with underwater sound recording equipment and sets it up. The sound that we hear changes when she turns the control knobs. The camera is close to the "aquanaut" and observes her actions: the devices render the sound of the marine organisms audible to the human ear and she mounts a sound event like a DJane. Connecting and tuning the channels, she is performing a submarine radio broadcast and transmits the sounds of the ocean into the ether. All of the creatures on Earth shall hear what happens in the depths of the oceans! Fluorescent sea butterflies swim toward us; they are very close, breathing. As a result of ocean acidification, these are microorganisms are endangered. The caption reads: "Their absence will silence the submarine springs."

In a kind of mythical chant, the woman takes up the concept of the destruction of the ecosystem and relates how the climate is changing for them, the Sami people. Climate changes lead to deaths of reindeer and as a result the ancient, symbiotic relationship between humans and animals – each other's guardians – is endangered. We hear her singing a Sami song off camera – a terrestrial echo of the oceanic sound, a cry into the ether. It is her contribution to making contact with the sea creatures. Again, she tunes her radio, and again goes on air. "That night, a few whales showed up near the surface." Maybe she did manage to establish communication, maybe not.

I chose the video *Acoustic Ocean* (2018) by Ursula Biemann as an introduction for a number of reasons. First of all, it supports my assertion that current techno-ecological and technofeminist perception has moved in the direction of relationships and communication with nonhuman natureculture[6] beings. In Biemann's fictive video, this occurs on an imaginary level: The technologies with which the protagonist operates function symbolically; the fish sounds come from an archive. However, the constructed setting does not interfere with our perception that a "real" situation might well be "documented" here. The protagonist uses the media of "nature" – the SOFAR water

---

6   To my knowledge, Donna Haraway suggested the term. It stands for hybrid assemblages of "nature," "culture," and "technology" beyond their dichotomies.

channel, the air, her voice, and her hands – to establish a different kind of communication. Technical means are also available, such as various recording and playback devices, computers, hydrophones, cables, and antennas. All of the media are equally important, of equal value. As a technoscientist and hybrid trickster with a headlamp and wearing orange, high-visibility clothing, she attempts to bring light into the darkness of the ocean and establish communication with its inhabitants. The boundaries between nature and culture and nature and technology dissolve. The media, as well as the female figure's clothing and makeup, stem from naturecultures. Hence the hydrophones, arranged in an octopus-like fashion, are to a lesser extent prosthesis-like techno-optimizations and instead "external organs that enable them to plunge deeply into the marine habitat." The boundaries of her body have also become indefinite. The watertight suit has sealable holes that enable an exchange with external environment. In this case, the outer space is nature, the habitat of human and nonhuman beings. A reindeer skin slung around the woman's neck testifies to the "aquanaut's" close ties to animals, an intimacy that not only implies scientific analysis or cuddlesome kinship, but also killing and consumption – since the ecology of coexistence also has to involve the provision of nourishment, the so-called food webs, that is, the complex interactions between the species that transport energy and nutritional value.[7] She also tells of these entangled chains and their disruption in her mythical chant. In fact, the question concerning the functioning of food chains and the provision of nourishment is not only primeval, but also current and impending. As Maria Puig de la Bellacasa points out, the threat of nourishing several billion people has been employed for decades to legitimize agro-industrial production and the colonization of land. At the same time, as she writes, it is precisely this accepted, shortsighted industrial agriculture that undermines current and future food security.

Acoustic Ocean documents the shift from technofeminism to techno-ecofeminism; for Ursula Biemann, it is a shift from issues of gender, globalization, and mobility to issues of raw materials, climate, and ecology. Her video essays, such as *Performing the Border* (1998)

---

7   Maria Puig de la Bellacasa points out that the food web concept examines not only who eats whom, but also how, for example, the waste of one species can provide nourishment for another. Puig de la Bellacasa, *Making Time for Soil*, p. 702.

and *Remote Sensing* (2001), framed explicitly cyberfeminist concerns. In times of a digital longing for the immaterial, they insisted on the materiality of bodies and raised what is in principle the ecofeminist question of the costs at which digital technologies arise and what genders subjectify them and how. Hierarchical divisions concerning the notions of body and nature lead to global inequities. In *Forest Law* (2014), a Native American in the Amazon fighting for the rights of the indigenous people relates that the rain forest does not constitute an outside-of-the-body for the people who live there, but is a part of it. His struggle for the rights of the Native Americans implies that international jurisprudence has to open itself up to concepts of physical existence that would include nonhuman beings.

Finally, the cyborg trickster figure appearing in *Acoustic Ocean* operates as an intermediary between the worlds and the new order of mutual awareness. She registers and *senses* what occurs around her with her *sensing* organs (sensing technologies). The figure is not a gendered signifier for the purpose of allegorically embodying the interests of others. She is "woman" but not specifically "female," a scientist as well as a singer; she is a human but also an indigenous Sami, a fish-like creature and an organ of her sensing machines. As a messenger of her own pluralities, she sets out to decolonize the technosciences and to initiate a cyborg requiem of the species: an underwater radio performance on video that combines different times, species, and atoms.

Conceptual Genealogies

In Ursula Biemann's last three videos – besides *Acoustic Ocean*, *Twenty One Percent* (2016) and *Subatlantic* (2015) – as in the early ones, "women" once more specifically come into play as the carriers and agents of knowledge. "Women" also play a prominent role in the artistic works I will discuss in the following. This brings "old" feminist concerns into play in a laid-back and casual way, namely that the deconstruction of hierarchical, dichotomous power structures means the participation of subjects who call themselves "women."

"In the 1990s, ecofeminists worked to remedy a perceived problem in feminist theory, animal advocacy, and environmentalism, namely, a lack of attention to the intersecting structures of power that reinforce the "othering" of women and animals, and contribute to the increasing destruction of the environment. Though sometimes called "utopian" or "concerned with too many issues," ecofeminist theory exposes and opposes intersecting forces of oppression, showing how problematic it is when these issues are considered separate from one another."[8] This statement brings home that techno-ecofeminist concerns go far beyond the apparently obligatory issues of gender, sex, and reproduction and take into account the economies of exploitation at work all over the world.

One of the foundations of feminist and queer deconstruction is the "queering" of powerful dichotomies. Feminists see this as the basic ideological and cultural structure for exploitation and subordination based on "othering," regardless of whether it is a matter of nature, gender, sex, disability, nonhuman beings, machines, and social, global or subaltern weaknesses. Those who help to break through these dualistic hierarchies in the direction of complex relations and entanglements of agents always take action, one could say, in a queer/ feminist or ecofeminist way: "Queer values – caring not (just) about the individual, the family, or one's own descendants, but about the Other species and persons to whom one has no immediate relations – may be the most effective ecological values."[9] Noticeably, the terms "feminism," "ecology" or, more up to date, "techno-ecology" are used universally. Whereas feminism works against power relations based on dichotomies, techno-ecology sees itself as a very fundamental theory of the collaboration of a wide range of agents who no longer give priority "only" to "green" concerns.

As Erich Hörl writes in the introduction to his anthology *General Ecology*: "Ecology has started to designate the collaboration of a multiplicity of human and nonhuman agents: it is something like the cipher of a new thinking of togetherness and of great cooperation of entities and forces, which has begun to be significant for contemporary thought; hence it forces and drives a radically relational onto-epistemological renewal."[10] Although one has to completely agree with Hörl on this observation and definition, it is nevertheless evident that the techno-ecological discourse, similar to the media-ecological discourse until not so long ago, strongly relies on networks based on technological media or the critique of the traditional concept of

---

8   Adams and Gruen, *Ecofeminism*, p. 1.

9   Nicole Seymore, quoted in Davies, *Toxic Progeny*, p. 232.

10 Hörl, *Introduction to General Ecology*, p. 3.

nature.[11] Concerns that have to do with the biosphere and imply relations with nonhuman beings are rarely fully differentiated. I repeat: Although the most innovative approaches with respect to new or "green" relations with naturecultures come from within feminist ranks, they are underrepresented in techno-ecological discourses. Of the fifteen authors in *General Ecology*, for example, only four of them are female, and that does not indicate whether their approaches are feminist. However, to the extent to which questions about coexistence, about animal and plant rights, empathy and care, repairing and healing are now starting to penetrate dominant theoretical and art discourses, feminist approaches have also left their ghettos. They are becoming key references where reformulations of coexistence are concerned: "Ecofeminist theory provides ethical guidance to challenge inequities arising along racial, gendered, and species boundaries."[12]

The Plastic Eaters and the Mermaid Torpedo

Relating to other forms of subjectivity has remained a major feminist concern to this day. The key figure of technofeminism was "the ironic myth" of the cyborg, which stands for the blurring of dual boundaries. Such a fluid body is to me a "symptom and effect body"; a body that displays the subject relations that produce it semiotically-materially.[13] What was new about it was, and cyberfeminists adopted these definitions, that cyborgs enjoy becoming a symptom and their boundaries becoming blurred. At the time I wrote: "Whereas feminism claimed the appropriation of new technologies as tools for women's liberation, cyberfeminism promotes both the idea of becoming cyborgian and the pleasures involved in it. In other words: technologies are no longer perceived as prostheses and instruments for liberation that are separated from the body... In cyberfeminism, the utopian ideology of women's liberation is located in the body and gender, but this body is no longer what it was thought to be."[14]

---

11 Broader approaches of media-ecology, however, not necessarily feminist ones, can be found, for example, in *The Fibreculture Journal*; *zfm*; Maxwell et.al., *Media and the Ecological Crisis*; Gabrys, *Program Earth*.

12 Adams and Gruen, *Ecofeminism*, p. 5.

13 Volkart, *Fluide Subjekte*, pp. 4–8.

14 Volkart, *The Cyberfeminist Fantasy of the Pleasure of the Cyborg*, pp. 99–100.

Fig. 3 (top): Pinar Yoldas: Plastic sensing organs, from:
Ecosystem of Excess

Fig. 4 (below): Pinar Yoldas: Plastic balloon-turtle, from:
Ecosystem of Excess

And further: "Resistance lays in the non/materiality of a constructed and discursive body itself."[15]

The concept of a material-semiotic, affective form of resistance formulated at the time became even more fully differentiated in the course of the "nonhuman turn" or the "material turn."[16] Matter is increasingly defined as vibrant, artefactual, and relational: "These vibrant animals, plants, viruses, hurricanes, storms, pharmaceuticals, and other technological artefacts vie with, make demands upon, and impede and enable human agency. They make their presence known to us, or, one could say, make "calls" to which we are continually responding," writes Jane Bennett.[17] Karen Barad also places emphasis on the relational, entangled, and reality-producing elements of her "agential realism." She writes: "Matter is not figured as a mere effect or product of discursive practices, but rather as an agentive factor in its iterative materialization."[18]

What is unique about cyberfeminism is that it included biological and chemical forces – for example, in the form of discarded female bodily fluids or dangerous viruses – in the concept of the performatively generated body in a playful (and not in every case unproblematic) way. Today, added to this are "environmental" and deep-time, geological, and physical conditions and their relational concatenations. The plastic-eating mutations in Pinar Yolda's project *Ecosystem of Excess* (2014), for instance, make reference to the geological non-expirability of plastic. They presage our future and play with the adaptability of "low" (nonhuman) organisms to environmental changes, something that for humans seems uncanny. "Nature," these miniature monsters say, always survives somehow. But is that what we want? The monstrous thing about the symptom and effect body of today consists in rendering Gaia's intrusion into the human sphere visible – to take up Stengers' concept – and in the shattering of the human perspective.

This also occurs in the two video projects *Sirenomelia* (2017) and *Mirror Matter Sirenomelia* (2017), in which the artist Emilija Škarnulyte plays a sea creature that swims through the dark, endless

---

15 Ibid. p. 100.

16 Cf. Grusin, *The Nonhuman Turn*.

17 Bennett, *Dynamische Materie und Zero Landscape*, p. 20; Bennett, "Vibrant Matter – Zero Landscape," p. 19

18 Barad, "Nature's Queer Performativity," p. 32.

Fig. 5 (top) and Fig. 6 (below): Video stills from Emilija Škarnulytė: Sirenomelia

channels and tunnels of a former NATO submarine base in the Arctic waters of Norway. "Sirenomelia," as she is called, is also the name of a condition, the so-called mermaid syndrome, a rare congenital deformity in which the legs are fused together Disease, disability, defect: those are the human perspectives on her silvery, shiny tail with which she agilely moves in this strange and uncanny underwater environment where the man-made, the technological, decays. Commandeered by sea anemones and other creatures, it thrives like a magical landscape. The two videos vary, above all with respect to how they begin: In the older work, for several minutes we see the slow-moving, rotating mountains of Svalbard, isolated by fragments of a white satellite dish. It is a geodesic telescope that measures the earth and the changes in the ocean caused by climate warming. We embark on a journey to the Arctic, a scientific expedition to an extreme place. By contrast, *Sirenomelia Mirror Matter* begins with a highly artificial, fluid mirror landscape and model-like techno-architecture – references to the artist's research residencies at the European Organization for Nuclear Research (CERN) in Geneva, and in Japan, where research stations have been built for the exploration of antimatter and mirror matter. In the video, they seem like scenes from a science fiction movie, suggesting that the figure came to Earth from the future. Both videos share hypnotic sounds and standstill; we look out at ice floes and a decapitated whale. Then the tunnels and basins, Sirenomelia swimming along, close to the marine creatures, as if she had to touch every millimeter. In the end we see how she "wags" out of the image, small, "disabled," floundering solitarily with what now seems to be her clumsy tail, all alone in the endlessly blue expanse.

Timothy Morton places emphasis on the cyborgian nature of Sirenomelia, her symptom and effect body, when he writes: "Emilija allows herself to be measured by cosmic and gigantic terrestrial forces: evolution, black holes, the biosphere, magnetic fields, photons, gravity waves, NATO, the Soviet Union, patriarchy, the military industrial complex, nuclear energy, crystals, minerals, the mineral extraction industry. She is a chameleon who lets herself be meditated on by beings that are physically larger than the conventional human realm, and which seem to many to be indifferent to it, or invisible, or irrelevant. But as we've seen, the reason why there's a radio telescope in the Artic is that things such as the biosphere and quasars have become relevant to human beings."[19]

---

19 Timothy Morton, "We Are All Mermaids," p. 8. Quasar means quasi-stellar radio wave and refers to the active center of a galaxy. Sonifications of quasar activity can be heard in the video.

There are not only various materializations, eras, and discourses combined in the Sirenomelia figure; she also mediates between them. She establishes contact with the strangely abandoned place as if she wanted to explore and testify to its vibrancy and connect the different spheres and elements with one another. The artist personally immerses herself in this situation. She "others"[20] – becomes fish, mermaid, submarine, torpedo, machine. But why a mermaid, of all things, this ancient male fantasy that has recently even provided the material for TV series for teenagers? As Emilija Škarnulyté told me, she wanted to strike out at this militarized place, which continues to tell of the disintegration of the myth of war, with a counter-myth: sea creatures have always been the mediators of "nature." They are not innocent; like the cyborgs, this makes them useful for paradoxical figurations: Sirenomelia comes from another space and another time; she is awkward, thrown in, the last survivor of a species or first one of its kind that is no longer human. She returns to that place from where life on Earth came: the water, in whose frigid temperatures she learned to live, to survive. Her "femaleness" is not accentuated; one does not see her hair. The camera's gaze concentrates on her movements, the way she glistens, the physical closeness and touch, but not on sex. Like Biemann's trickster figure, Sirenomelia is also a mediator that establishes a different kind of communication and participation. Her body, this contradictory assemblage consisting of ages, matters, gestures, and fantasies, is a signal from the future that establishes contact without the great gesture of appropriation and colonization. What remains are traces – waves on the surface of the water.

To Mother a Plant:
A Special Kind of Care

According to Špela Petrič, the technoscientific mentality of feasibility determines our perception of nonhuman organisms. Earth has become a laboratory – an experiment with an unknown outcome. We are within it, and because of this we have to take action if other relations want to be established. Petrič therefore constructs test arrangements, takes "the laboratory" into public space, and makes it – under

---

20 On the concept of "othering" as a subject-changing process, see Adorf, *Operation Video*.

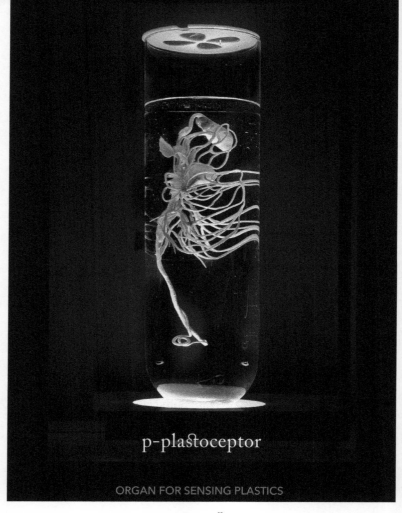

Fig. 7 (top) and Fig. 8 (below): Špela Petrič: Phytoteratology

other, aesthetic premises – negotiable. For her project *Phytoteratology* (2017), it was a question of a different form of procreating, breeding, and care." I wanted to mother a plant, a gentle green alien," emphasizing that the dominant idea of fathering is replaced by that of maternal-monstrous engendering/mothering. For the project, she extracted embryonic tissue from a so-called weed and nourished it in an incubator with steroids from her own urine. With reference to the reproduction method of this plant, this means artificial conception and subsequently the blending of the vegetal tissue with human cells: While from the outside seemingly "normal," the product is a transspecies plant that was crossed on a morphological level. Petrič apparently repeats strategies of molecular biology and the associated blurring of boundaries, which is common practice in technoscience today and for which there are few ethical guidelines. Do her actions frighten us because they intervene more deeply than traditional practices of breeding, namely on a molecular level, or because she blends the human-plant species? Or because her method illustrates that with technosciences even conventional or "normal" breeding methods acquire the overtone of exploitation, optimization, and unpredictable experiment? Špela Petrič presents the incubators with the growing plants in the exhibition space along with a video; the installation is accompanied by a performance in which such questions are raised.

Phytoteratology makes a case for the necessity of broadening the current discourse on genetic engineering and biotechnologies. It can no longer be just a matter of the dichotomy between human and plant; rather, the question must be asked concerning what power relations and economies code what kind of nonhuman entities, and who benefits from it. It becomes clear that other relationships could be established under laboratory conditions: "There are very different kinds of care," she says.[21] "These tiny monsters, coming into being from an impossible love, with intense labor and a yearning of plant parenthood, emerge in a time of environmental, political and social crisis as beings of permeability, harbingers of affective agential intra-action. Making kin with plants, caring for us, hopeful monsters."[22] With these concepts, Petrič takes up Barad's and Haraway's arguments, both of whom do not fundamentally come out either for or against

---

21 Špela Petrič in conversation with Yvonne Volkart, April 2018.
22 On this, see the website http://www.spelapetric.org//portfolio/ectogenesis.

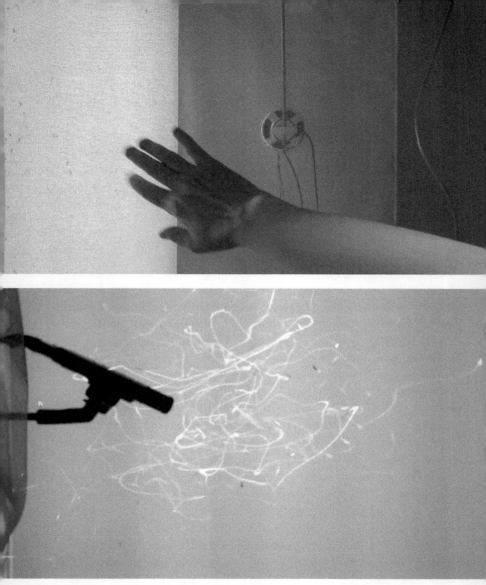

Fig. 9 (top) and Fig. 10 (bottom): Ursula Damm: Insect Songs

synthetic biology and biotechnology.[23] Taking care of others in times of technoscience is a challenge that has to be repeatedly readdressed and continuously performed, so that it does not remain abstract. It cannot, as another project by Petrič revealed, always succeed.[24] Also in this project, the elements of love, care, and shared time, which were at work for several months in the beginning of the project, are not fully presented in the quite technical set-up of the exhibition. The now "motherless" plants remained somehow "alone" and therefore could not thrive in this difficult environment. And yet, Petrič's experiments set themselves apart from that "human" hubris of technological feasibility into which xenofeminism à la Laboria Cuboniks lapses, when they say: "If nature is unjust, change nature!"[25] The old feminist work on the concept of nature does not simply imply the one-sided control of "nature," but a vibrant balancing of differently oriented "queer" relations.

Meaning-less Communication

I would like to conclude the discussion of artistic projects with a performance and its documentation on film in which "real" communication between mosquitos, humans, musical instruments, and various media technologies are established. The point of departure for the project was an experience that the artist had: She began to miss the sound of insects. Her research revealed that in Germany alone, 75 percent of the insect population has disappeared. The exact causes are not yet known; it can presumably be traced back to pesticides, as well as to the loss of their natural habitats.

In *Insect Songs* (2018) by Ursula Damm in collaboration with Christina Meißner (cello) and Teresa Carrasco (sound), we see, and above all hear, tentative, soft, or screeching sounds, overtones, pure tones; a woman playing the cello, whirring and buzzing, mosquitoes can be seen on a monitor; their flight paths are being recorded, and there is also a box in which they fly around, confined. The

---

23 This openness also led to ecofeminist critique, for example by Donovan, "Participatory Epistemology, Sympathy, and Animal Ethics," pp. 87–88.

24 See my critique of this in *Does Art Make a Difference? Technologies of the Ecological after the Anthropocene*, pp. 154–57.

25 Laboria Cuboniks, *Xenofeminism*, p. 34.

performance is meant to bring about an experimental situation, in which it is first of all possible to observe whether and how mosquitos react to music played by people and instruments and what the later results might be. The intention is to create a kind of dialogue and engagement-with-one-another, namely with those seemingly annoying animals whose disappearance people normally desire more than they would later regret. The performance was preceded by years of preparation, during which the artist made an "arena" in her kitchen using "biomedia," such as gauze, glass, yeast, and wine, which attracted flying insects and enticed them to perform a courting dance and song. She recorded the sound that was produced in the process. In collaboration with the neuroscientist Birgit Brüggemeier, software was developed that detects the pitch of the mosquito songs and amplifies and modulates the sounds that occur. What results is a song similar to human music.

First, a technical set up enabling hearing and seeing the insects' flight paths was created. The cellist Christina Meißner was asked to improvise to it and find out what sounds cause a change in their behavior. For the subsequent recording, Meißner wanted to work exclusively by way of listening and attempted, according to her understanding, to produce mosquito sounds, and in doing so entice the mosquitoes into swarming. It became apparent from the very beginning that the mosquitoes were engaging in this interaction. Ursula Damm wrote: "The type of music is as amorphous as our perception of mosquito song. It does not correspond with our music habits but enters a stage of sound perception that is more primal, raw, simple. First of all, a part of the process is to find the species-specific tone/pitch, to see if overtones have an effect, and later in the piece also effectuate the musician's abandon as a human being in a dialogue. Christina Meißner did not want to force the mosquitoes to react; rather, she wanted to "become a mosquito" herself and "sing with them'."[26] And she continued: "The actual media-related aspect is that we humans have to become quiet in order to hear the mosquitoes. Admittedly, we use technology to enable us to hear them, and we in turn use technology to examine the impact our music has on the mosquitoes."[27] But they are simple arrangements, not sensors: "For me it is an aesthetic decision not to employ any additional technology,

---

26 Ursula Damm, e-mail to Yvonne Volkart, May 2018.
27 Ibid.

but to work on my attentiveness (being quiet, watching at length) or to simulate the habitat of the mosquitos (mosquito box). Instead of being about technology, it is about understanding the different "Umwelten" [surrounding worlds] in the sense of Jakob Johann von Uexküll. To me, making music together with feedback on and responding to the reaction seems to be much more than merely working with sensors. One senses and develops meaning for one another. If you rely on feedback, you save yourself the step of technical data production + interpretation + application."[28]

The extraordinary thing about this work is the fact that we attain an independent temporality of listening through the unpredictable, "interactively" arranged timing of the sound, the foreignness of the tones, and the self-imposed concentration and quietness. As Christoph Brunner has shown, aesthetic timing, as the experienced and shared time in the here and now, provides the condition for what he, in connection with Brian Massumi, calls the "ecology of relation."[29] What is meant by this is a specific form of temporality that touches those present on an affective level and "calls on" them in their physicality and relationship to others in the room as a plurality of pre-individual entities in embryo, in this case: faces, flies, sounds, movements, technologies, signals, traces, and so on. The abandon experienced by each individual in this event, which extends over a longer period of time without a specifically announced beginning or end, becomes a consciously perceived experience of shared participation; Ursula Damm speaks of "shared experience" or "shared habitats." This is based on communication that initially appears to be completely meaningless because it is situated outside of our language codes and, for us, serves no apparent purpose. However, this communication becomes meaningful if it can involve a different kind of "understanding," empathy, and collectively created and shared (temporary) temporality. In this sense it provides an aesthetic excess of pure becoming and goes beyond any purposeful rationality – a hierarchical relationship that in the context of "green" lifestyles people readily pursue in their contacts with nonhuman creatures.[30]

---

28 Ibid.

29 Cf. Brunner, *Affective Politics of Timing.*

30 In the same way "women" are not automatically feminists, an "organic label" does not rule out exploitation.

In Favor of a Techno-Eco-Queer-Feminist Being-with-Others

The examples discussed show that the irony of cyberfeminism has changed into an aesthetic of participation and participating that does not shy away from developing empathy toward, and affective relationships with, nonhuman creatures and also staging them aesthetically. The building and fostering of such relations is associated with a great deal of effort, personal as well, and cannot be substituted with technological optimizations. The idea that human beings caringly or even healingly intervene in what industrial economies destroy no longer seems ridiculous or lame.[31] On the contrary, such values contribute to the erosion of the dualism of "human" versus "nature" or "good" versus "evil" discussed above and which, for example, continue to be perpetuated in xenofeminism. Modes of coexistence are invented that are commensurate with the seriousness of the situation in the Anthropocene. Natasha Myers writes that what is cultivated is a "robust mode of knowing grounded in queer, feminist, decolonial politics."[32] Christoph Brunner speaks of an "ecology of relation": "From pure relationality to an ecology of relation, an amplification takes place which selects out of the manyness of potential lines several without disregarding the others. This process is politically relevant because an ecology does not mark an already closed system but gives forces the potential to actively attune to an emergent situation, 'in the name of that which emerges.'"[33]

Becoming involved in the diverse ecology of relations reveals that there are different temporalities and spatialities. Maria Puig de la Bellacasa writes that from the perspective of an earthworm, catalyst

---

31 Theorists such as Donna Haraway, Maria Puig de la Bellacasa, Vinciane Despret, Lori Gruen, Natasha Myers, and Anna Lowenhaupt Tsing, or permaculture design in general, make reference to "healing" aspects in a positive way. Haraway writes about fictions in which it is about "migrat[ing] to ruined places and work[ing] with human and non-human partners to heal these places... Donna Haraway, *Staying with the Trouble*, p. 137.

32 Myers, https://catalystjournal.org/index.php/catalyst/article/view/28848/pdf_17, p. 1.

33 Ibid.

fertilizers are growth inhibitors.[34] If we allow this involvement of different times, spaces, and factors, it becomes apparent that accelerationist strategies fall short, because they are conceived too "humanly": They emanate from a dualism of temporality and the exclusivity of the capitalist production paradigm, which in view of the emergence of the forces and range of unpredictable transformations is untenable.

Unfortunately, limiting and limited perspectives of this kind dominate contemporary rhetoric and policy, even though they are so obviously recognizable as phantasmal constructions in their adherence to anthropocentric hubris. Isabelle Stengers has repeatedly pointed out that it is necessary to challenge such powerful simplicities, for example by beginning to ask simple and concrete questions. Questions are difficult to answer because things are more complicated than they are made out to be.[35] Transversal practices need to be invented and lived: imaginary, aesthetic, activist practices – life practices. Practices that, on any level, create an excess of meaning, a not-being-wrapped-up in the limitations of capitalist, dual argumentations. Techno-ecofeminist queerings – to the extent that, as I asserted at the beginning, activate the vibrancy, transformational power, and relationality of human and nonhuman entities and their different temporalities – seem more than suitable for this purpose: "Queer attachments work both to celebrate the excess of life and to politicize the sites at which this excess is eradicated."[36]

Bibliography

Adams, Carol J., and Lori Gruen. *Ecofeminism: Feminist Intersections with Other Animals and the Earth*. New York and London: Bloomsbury, 2014.

Adorf, Sigrid. *Operation Video: Eine Technik des Nahsehens und ihr spezifisches Subjekt; die Videokünstlerin der 1970er Jahre*. Bielefeld: transcript, 2008.

Avanessian, Armen, and Helen Hester, eds. *dea ex machina*. Berlin: Merve, 2015.

Barad, Karen. "Nature's Queer Performativity." *Kvinder* 1, no. 2, pp. 25-53.

Bennett, Jane. *Vibrant Matter. A Political Ecology of Things*, Durham: Duke University Press, 2010.

---

34 Puig de la Bellacasa, *Making Time for Soil*, p. 709.

35 Stengers, *In Catastrophic Times*.

36 Catriona Mortimer-Sandilands and Burce Erickson, *Queer Ecologies*, quoted in Davies, *Toxic Progeny*, p. 232.

Bennett, Jane, and Klaus K. Loenhart. "Vibrant Matter, Zero Landscape: Interview with Jane Bennett. *GAM* 07 (October 19, 2011) pp. 14-25.

Brunner, Christoph. "Affective Politics of Timing: On Emergent Collectivity in Ragnar Kjartansson's *The Visitors*." In Marie-Luise Angerer et al., eds. *Timing of Affect: Epistemologies, Aesthetics, Politics*. Berlin and Zurich: diaphanes, 2014, pp. 245-62.

Coole, Diana. "Der neue Materialismus: Die Ontologie und die Politik der Materialisierung." In Susanne Witzgall and Kerstin Stakemeier, eds. *Macht des Materials / Politik der Materialität*. Zurich: diaphanes, 2014, pp. 29-46.

Davies, Heather. "Toxic Progeny: The Plastisphere and Other Queer Futures." *philoSOPHIA: A Journal of Continental Feminism* 5, no. 2 (Summer 2015), pp. 231-50.

Davies, Heather, and Etienne Turpin, eds. *Art in the Anthropocene: Encounters Among Aesthetics, Politics, Environments and Epistemologies*. Ann Arbor: Open Humanities Press, 2015.

Donovan, Josephine. "Participatory Epistemology, Sympathy, and Animal Ethics." In Carol J. Adams and Lori Gruen, eds. *Ecofeminism: Feminist Intersections with Other Animals and the Earth*. London: Bloomsbury, 2014, pp. 75-90.

The Fibreculture Journal. Issue 17: *Unnatural Ecologies* (April 21, 2011). fibreculture-journal.org

Gabrys, Jennifer. *Program Earth: Environmental Sensing Technology and the Making of a Computational Planet*. Minneapolis and London: Universtiy of Minnesota Press, 2016.

Grusin, Richard, ed. *Anthropocene Feminism*. Minneapolis and London: Universtiy of Minnesota Press, 2017.

Grusin, Richard. *The Nonhuman Turn*. Minneapolis and London: Universtiy of Minnesota Press, 2015.

Guattari, Félix. *The Three Ecologies*. Translated by Ian Pindar and Paul Sutton. London and New Brunswick, NJ: The Athlone Press, 2000.

Haraway, Donna. "The Promises of Monsters: A Regenerative Politics for Inappropriate/d Others. In Lawrence Grossberg, Cary Nelson, and Paula Treichler, eds. *Cultural Studies*. New York: Routledge, 1992, pp. 295–337.

Haraway, Donna. *Staying with the Trouble: Making Kin in the Chthulucene*. Durham, NC: Duke University Press, 2016.

Laboria Cuboniks. *Xenofeminism: A Politics for Alienation*. http://www.laboriacuboniks.net/20150612

Lowenhaupt Tsing, Anna: *The Mushroom at the End of the World: On the Possibility of Life in Capitalist Ruins*. Princeton and Oxford: Princeton University Press, 2015.

Precarias a la Deriva. "Globalisierte Sorge." In Tobias Bärtsch et al., eds. Ökologien *der Sorge*. Vienna: transversal texts, 2017, pp. 25–96. http://transversal.at/books/ oekologiendersorge.

Puig de la Bellacasa, Maria. "Making Time for Soil: Technoscientific Futurity and the Pace of Care." *Social Studies of Science* 45 (2015), pp. 692–716.

Maxwell, Richard, Jon Raundalen, and Nina Lager Vestberg, eds. *Media and the Ecological Crisis*. New York and London: Routledge, 2015.

Myers, Natasha. "Ungrid-able Ecologies: Decolonzing the Ecological Sensorium in a 10,000 year-old NaturalCultural Happening." *Catalyst: Feminism, Theory, Technoscience* 3, no. 3 (2017), p. 1–24. http://www.catalystjournal.org.

Morton, Timothy. "We Are All Mermaids." Manuscript for the exhibition *Manifold* at Decad in Berlin, June 22–August 26, 2017. Berlin, 2017

Neimanis, Astrida. *Bodies of Water*. London: Bloomsbury, 2017.

Stengers, Isabelle. *In Catastrophic Times: Resisting the Coming Barbarism*. Translated by Andrew Goffey. Lüneburg: Open Humanities Press in collaboration with meson press, 2015.

The Laboratory Planet. No. 5: *Alien Capitalism* (2016).

Weinstein, Jami, and Claire Colebrook, eds. *Posthumous Life: Theorizing Beyond the Posthuman*. New York: Columbia University Press, 2017.

Volkart, Yvonne. *Fluide Subjekte: Anpassung und Widerspenstigkeit in der Medienkunst*. Bielefeld: transcript, 2006.

Volkart, Yvonne. "The Cyberfeminist Fantasy of the Pleasure of the Cyborg." In Claudia Reiche and Verena Kuni, eds. *Cyberfeminism: Next Protocols*. New York: Autonomedia, 2004.

Volkart, Yvonne. "Does Art Make a Difference? Technologies of the Ecological After the Anthropocene." In Rasa Smite and Raitis Smits, eds. *Acoustic Space*. Issue 17: *Open Fields, Art and Science Research Practices in the Network Society*. Riga: RIXC, 2018, pp. 149_64.

zfm: Zeitschrift für Medienwissenschaften. Issue 4: *Medienökologien* (January 2016).

The ongoing research project "Ecodata-Ecomedia-Ecoaesthetics," which is being conducted at the Institute of Aesthetic Practice and Theory, Academy of Art and Design FHNW Basel (2017-20) and produced these results, was made possible by funding provided by the Swiss National Foundation.

STIRRING THE EMBERS

Preliminary Critical Notes on Xenofeminisms

Isabel de Sena

THE XENOFEMINIST MANIFESTO – OFFICIALLY, "XENOFEMINSIM: A Politics for Alienation" – was first published online in 2014 as the brainchild of the polyglossial collective Laboria Cuboniks, composed of Amy Ireland (Sydney), Diann Bauer (London), Helen Hester (London), Katrina Burch (nomadic), Lucca Fraser (Halifax), and Patricia Reed (Berlin). A logic- and reason-embracing mutant of left-accelerationism re-engineered with cyberfeminist genes, xenofeminism (XF) is described as a "technomaterialist, anti-naturalist, and gender abolitionist form of feminism."[1] Its aim is "to articulate

---

1 Hester, H. (2018), *Xenofeminism*. Medford, Cambridge: Polity Books, p.6.

a feminism fit for the twenty-first century."[2] Its motto: "If nature is unjust, change nature!" (OVERFLOW, 0x1A).[3]

Hailed by critics, XF has been said to "definitively grasp feminism back from the ... hands of the moralizing-spiteful petit-bourgeoisie."[4] Also among the general public – if Google is anything to go by – but also in witnessing the newly spawned "disciple movements" or the wave of XF (over-) representation at public events in cities like Berlin and London – there seems to be a choir of univocal accolade verging on glorification for all things XF. It is difficult, even four years on, to find critical voices. This is at best surprising, given some of the distinctly audacious – alternatively, brash and ill considered – claims of XF. At worst, it is also detrimental to XF. Itself aiming to be "a platform, an incipient ambition to construct a new language ... that seizes its own methods as materials to be reworked" (OVERFLOW, 0x19), one would assume consensus is not exactly the lifeblood they were hoping for.

This text aims to stir the embers somewhat, to open a new conversation on XF by addressing a number of fundamental tenets it adopts which I argue are untenable, specifically their conceptualizations of scalability and universality. This critique is by no means exhaustive; it comprises an initial and partial instigation to challenge a publication that though provocative, has subsisted without the oppositional voices that might invigorate the discourse around it. Given the confusing and confused nature of the concepts, but also in a genuine spirit to invite response, the discussions are each translated into a series of questions. The analysis is guided by a number of seminal feminist texts published between 1984 and 2015, which not only offer a direct retaliation to the three concepts mentioned above, but also show their teeth, muscles, and sinews as vigorous narratives from the past and present of feminist practice. In their undying commitment to

2   Laboria Cuboniks (2018), *The Xenofeminist Manifesto: A Politics for Alienation*. London: Verso Books.

3   *Xenofeminsim: A Politics for Alienation*, laboriacuboniks.net. Quotations from the manifesto are referenced by noting their heading (an imperative verb) and subheading (a number and/or letter combination comprising a consecutive series).

4   Mark Fisher quoted in: "After Accelerationism: The Xenofeminist Manifesto," tripleampersand.org (June 11, 2015).

non-scalability and non-universality, they are quite comfortably invulnerable to being qualified as "petit-bourgeois."

// SCALABILITY

The XF Manifesto states, "Refusing to think beyond the micro community … to consider how emancipatory tactics can be scaled up for universal implementation, is to remain satisfied with temporary and defensive gestures" (TRAP, 0x0A). It consequently coalesces "the unambitious and the non-scalable" (ADJUST, 0x11), asserting the wish to tear them down.

It will not be unreasonable here to consider for a moment why exactly so many proficient scholars and practitioners have come to reject scalability, consistently and over several decades now. The concept in fact is plagued by a number of fundamental problems that, together with their particular histories and disciplinary ancestries, cannot simply be bypassed. In the XF manifesto, the concept is mystifyingly abstract, lacking any form of address of these important details, which leaves unclear whether Laboria Cuboniks adheres to the concept regardless of its implications, or whether its militant adherence to it obviates a thorough lack of consideration.

Anthropologist Anna Lowenhaubt Tsing is among those who have dedicated rigorous thought to the issue, of which she offers a concise diagnosis in chapter three of "The Mushroom at the End of the World," titled "Some Problems with Scale." Cutting to the chase already in the first paragraph, she states the problem with scalability is primarily that it "demands the possibility of infinite expansion without changing the research framework … the research questions … [or] the framing assumptions."[5] These stakes seem rather high for something as trite as "infinite expansion." However, history clearly disagrees: In its steadfast nature, and unyieldingness to the details of processual alterations, scalability has become the darling of (mainstream) modern science, lending it the ideal methodological framework to make sweeping universal claims. Unsurprisingly, science has since centuries and to great avail adopted scalability as one of its fundamental requirements, and discarded as irrelevant (like XF) any projects that don't comply with

---

5   Tsing, A.L., p.38.

it. It is gainful to ignore the reality of interruption – to "admit only data that already fit the research frame."[6]

To be clear, these are not possible, optional, or even probable characteristics of scalability; they are its non-negotiable prerequisites. Scalability is unachievable unless a project's fundamental components are made perfectly uniform (and therefore transposable) and hermetically immutable to any adaptation-requiring details encountered along the way. That is what scalability *means*. Hence, it is scalability that is essentially conformist – in the fundamental sense of the word, "to 'make (something) like another thing'"[7] – while non-scalability essentially is not. Change and transformation are the mortal enemies of scalability; they are toxic to it; it withers and dies in their fumes.

And of course, the lucrativeness of scalability extends beyond the field of science. In its bull-headed pursuit of maximally efficient – i.e., homogeneous, identically replicable – growth, scalability deserves full credit for making projects profitable and for this reason has become the *modus operandi* of many an exploitative endeavor. As a characteristic and precondition of all progress narratives, it has come to define – and capacitate – the machinery of capitalism. In the context of capitalism, Laboria Cuboniks' adherence to scalability comes as no surprise. As an accelerationist spin-off, it aims to cannibalize the instruments/systems of capitalism, thereby taking distance from the self-sanctity of leftist politics. This it has made clear, consistently and on numerous platforms, including the manifesto, and the appropriationist impulse is both clear and valid. However, as gender studies scholar Emma Rees observes, "any potential for scalability and real-world application that xenofeminism might have remains frustratingly elusive," which makes it very difficult to say anything about how Laboria Cuboniks envisions scalable projects might possibly circumvent the problems outlined above, if this is at all the intention.[8]

Seeking an example elsewhere will at least provide a foothold and is anyhow crucial in view of historical awareness; as stated in the manifesto, "we not should not hesitate to learn from ... the successes and failures of history" (PARITY, 0x10). The first scalable project, for

---

6   Idem.

7   Conform (n.d.), in: *Google Dictionary* (accessed 22.05.2018).

8   Rees, E., "Xenofeminism, by Helen Hester," in: www.timeshighereducation.com/books/review-xenofeminism-helen-hester-polity-press (March 1, 2018).

instance, is the landscape model that emerged from the 16th-17th century European colonial plantation. The Portuguese in Brazil were the first to stumble on this golden "formula for smooth expansion" and developed the alienated, isolated, extracted, abstracted, self-contained, standardizable, interchangeable – and therefore commodifiable – project elements that have come to define scalability.[9] The process leading up to this achievement went "as follows: Exterminate local people and plants; prepare now-empty, unclaimed land; and bring in exotic and isolated labor and crops for production."[10] This model "became an inspiration for later industrialization and [capitalist] modernization"[11]; the property of scalability on which it is based has made possible the full-blown exploitation of people and resources that has become the gruesomely common new normal in the realities of many, past and present.

Again: How does Laboria Cuboniks propose to *practice* scalability in a way that does not fall back on its *inherently* exploitative patterns, as evidenced by this and a myriad of other historic and contemporary examples? There is little to no discussion within their very abstracted address of the concept – in which they neglect to situate it both epistemologically (i.e., in relation to science) and historically (i.e., in relation to the colonial plantation that birthed it and the many other exploitative infrastructures that followed) – to how exactly they envision a *practicable* implementation of the oxymoron that is adaptive, diversified scalability.

This does seem to be their intention. In the manifesto, Laboria Cuboniks explicitly rejects many of the implications of scalability outlined above. For instance, they claim to "invite contamination as a mutational driver" (CARRY, 0x17) and state that "the task of engineering platforms for social emancipation and organization cannot ignore the cultural and semiotic mutations these platforms afford" (TRAP, 0x0D). It appears then, that Laboria Cuboniks wants to adopt scalability therein aligning itself with mainstream modern science and even more closely with the notion of progress epitomized in capitalism, but repudiates admitting the *inherent* conditions of scalability

9   Tsing, A.L., p.39.
10 Idem.
11 Idem.

to its project. Of course, however, they cannot have their cake and eat it, too.

So is the scalability they propose to practice in fact *not scalability*? And if not, why call it that? If they mean developing work that reaches many people or operates on otherwise large scales, why not say that: "develop large-scale projects"? Not as catchy, admittedly, but certainly more accurate. In any case, developing large-projects is not the same as "scalability," which simply makes it quite senseless to call it so.

Alternatively, if the scalability they propose *is scalability*, how do they account for the fact that the processes of abstraction, isolation, and standardization that are necessarily implicated in any scalable project are essentially incompatible with the ideas of mutability and contamination they advance, or for the fact they effectively hijack any possibility for *social* emancipation, leaving only space for top-down, autocratic and delusional hallucinations of a *gifted* emancipation, i.e., no emancipation at all?

On a final note, Tsing is quick to stress that "it would be a huge mistake to assume that scalability is bad and non-scalability is good. Non-scalable projects can be as terrible in their effects as scalable ones." Non-scalable projects therefore do not at all escape scrutiny; there is no intrinsic sanctity whatsoever in them. As she explains, "The main distinguishing feature between scalable and non-scalable projects is not ethical conduct, but rather that the latter are more diverse because they are not geared up for expansion."[12] The main – and inevitable – consequence of XF's adoption of scalability as a key driver, assuming scalability is indeed what they mean, is therefore that it "banishes meaningful diversity, that is, diversity that might change things."[13]

// UNIVERSALITY

The manifesto claims, that "XF constructs ... a future in which the realization of gender justice and feminist emancipation contribute to a universalist politics assembled from the needs of every human" (ZERO, 0x00) and "declares the right of everyone to speak as no one in particular" (ZERO, 0x04).

---

12 Idem., p.41.
13 Idem., p.38.

This is immediately reminiscent of two seminal feminist texts. The first is Donna Haraway's 1988 essay, "Situated Knowledges: The Science Question in Feminism and the Privilege of Partial Perspective." Specifically, it is reminiscent of the notion of "the god trick" – famously introduced in this essay – by which Haraway refers to the illusionist deception that for centuries has allowed "The imagined 'they'" of [masculine] objectivity in science to "leap out the marked body and into a conquering gaze": The trick "of seeing everything from nowhere."[14] It is difficult to see how speaking "as no one in particular," or assuming to speak for "every human" is not a re-performance of this god trick, now under the seemingly unified guise of "feminist emancipation." Which feminist emancipation? *Whose* feminist emancipation? The combination of a self-evident, universal "we" with this singular subject begs many questions.

As Haraway continues, in her attack on universalism through her insistence on "the particularity and embodiment of all vision," "where partiality and not universality is the condition of being heard to make rational knowledge claims," and in her mission in this essay to outline a *feminist objectivity*, which "means quite simply *situated knowledges*," Haraway finds no exemption for "The positionings of the subjugated."[15] These are no more "'innocent' positions" than those of the patriarch or any other "master decoder," but rather "knowledgeable modes of denial through repression, forgetting, and disappearing acts – ways of being nowhere while claiming to see comprehensively."[16] To assume the first person plural voice of a mythically singular "feminist emancipation" with the sweeping universalist and ventriloquist gesture to "speak for every human" is to neglect that, which might actually produce "better accounts of the world," namely "webs of differential positionings," of "limited location," and "the joining of partial views ... of views from somewhere."[17] Much more can be said, but there is little need for it; "The moral is simple: Only partial perspective promises objective vision. It allows us to become answerable."[18]

14 Haraway, D., pp.575, 581.

15 Idem., pp.582, 584, 589.

16 Idem., pp.584, 593.

17 Idem., pp.583, 590.

18 Idem., p.583.

That is the core issue at stake: Accountability. The ensuing question is how Laboria Cuboniks proposes to possibly – and again, *if at all* – make itself *accountable* if the politics it undertakes is universalist, and if it supports everyone's right (including their own) to speak from the abstracted, alienated position of *no body in particular*, while taking it upon itself to construct a future feminist emancipation that miraculously subsumes the needs of every body?

Laboria Cuboniks dedicates an entire paragraph in the manifesto to nuancing their notion of universality, which in its relevance to this discussion deserves full mention:

"Xenofeminism understands that the viability of emancipatory abolitionist projects – the abolition of class, gender, and race – hinges on a profound reworking of the universal. The universal must be grasped as generic, which is to say, intersectional. Intersectionality is not the morcellation of collectives into a static fuzz of cross-referenced identities, but a political orientation that slices through every particular, refusing the crass pigeonholing of bodies. This is not a universal that can be imposed from above, but built from the bottom up – or, better, laterally, opening new lines of transit across an uneven landscape. This non-absolute, generic universality must guard against the facile tendency of conflation with bloated, unmarked particulars – namely Eurocentric universalism – whereby the male is mistaken for the sexless, the white for raceless, the cis for the real, and so on. Absent such a universal, the abolition of class will remain a bourgeois fantasy, the abolition of race will remain a tacit white-supremacism, and the abolition of gender will remain a thinly veiled misogyny, even – especially – when prosecuted by avowed feminists themselves." (PARITY, 0x0F)

The first question is how much universality is left in this universal. A "non-absolute" universal might be said to be yet another oxymoron, in which case the same question arises as for scalability: Why call it so if it is not? More importantly, however – admitting for the sake of argument that such a universal is possible, which in fact is certainly arguable, albeit not convincingly addressed in the text – the second question is how this universal actually takes shape in *practice*, and whether XF succeeds in its ambitious "reworking of the universal" as "a political orientation that slices through every particular," despite its abstracting tendencies. What follows addresses these questions by returning to the core issue of accountability and extending it to an examination of how exactly the universal substantiates in the manifesto.

Poet and radical feminist Adrienne Rich in her seminal lecture for the "Conference on Women, Feminist Identity, and Society in the 1980s" held in Utrecht, the Netherlands in 1984, titled "Notes toward a Politics of Location," offers additional thoughts on the issue of accountability. Especially, she addresses the inevitable compromise of accountability in the face of disembodiment, or of the "faceless, raceless, classless category of 'all women'," under the "'deadly sameness' of abstraction," which she is not tongue-tied to designate as a "creation of white Western self-centeredness."[19] No, Laboria Cuboniks does not speak for "all women." But "every human" is equally if not more faceless, raceless, and classless; as is the abstracted, singular, fantastical category of "feminist emancipation"; as is the chronically recurrent and deeply mystifying "we" with which the text is permeated: "[I]t is imperative that *we* develop an ideological infrastructure," "*we* must overhaul," "*we* must engineer," "How are *we* to become," "How do *we* build," "the desires *we* want," "the problems *we* face," "*We* should," "*We* need," "*we* see," and so on and so forth. Who is "*we*"? And why is it speaking for "*us*"?

Is "we" everyone, everywhere? Or is it everyone in the West? Or just the feminists? All of them, or just the technofeminists, or rather the cyberfeminists? Is it Western feminists? Does "we" include feminists in rural communities in large swathes of Asia, Africa, and Central/South America, for instance, who have no privileged access to technology? What role is there for them to play within Laboria Cuboniks' self-ascribed task of constructing the future through "The radical opportunities afforded by developing (and alienating) forms of technological mediation"? Laboria Cuboniks explicitly recognizes that "no one can claim [digital tools'] comprehensive accessibility." But in noting that most of "the world's poor is adversely affected by the expanding technological industry" takes it upon itself to combat "these conditions as a target for elimination" (all: INTERRUPT, 0X08). So is the role of feminists in these communities limited to being saved?

Who knows – one can only guess at a faceless face. But while the "we" is left unnamed, there are clues in the text about who is not included. They show how Laboria Cuboniks' abstracted disengagement from its own limited localities and its megalomaniac ambitions to speak for all evidence an inconsideration of political accountability,

---

19 Rich, A., pp.219, 221.

and thereby a renunciation of objectivity, specifically feminist objectivity. For example, on the topic of the family, they state:

"We see too well that reinventions of family structure and domestic life are currently only possible at the cost of either withdrawing from the economic sphere – the way of the commune – or bearing its burdens manifold – the way of the single parent. If we want to break the inertia that has kept the moribund figure of the nuclear family unit in place … we must overhaul the material infrastructure and break the economic cycles that lock it in place."

Clearly, "The task before *us*" is in any case not that of the millions of people living in the polygamy belt stretching across sub-Saharan Africa, "from Senegal through to Tanzania, in which it is not uncommon for a third of married women to share their husbands."[20] This whole section of the planet – and many others, in which the Western trend of the nuclear family is by far the *minority* family structure – recognizes nothing in the two singular, "only" options described above: *either withdrawing from the economic sphere or bearing its burdens manifold*. Rather, their domestic realities are shaped by the far more common structure of the extended family – and the particular set of problems that derive from it – which includes parent(s) and kin from outside the nuclear family, and is common not only in sub-Saharan Africa, but also in large parts of Asia, the Middle East, and Central and South America.[21] That is a substantial part of the global population whose realities are left unaddressed in this manifesto for the future. And who are nevertheless subsumed into a "we" who outlines the problems "we" face and defines the solutions "we" should seek. This fails to account for the unspoken yet undeniably *practiced* assumption, articulated by Rich already in 1984, "That only certain kinds of people can make theory; that the white-educated mind is capable of formulating everything; that white middle-class feminism can know for "all women"; that only when a white mind formulates is the formulation to be taken seriously."[22]

---

20 Fenske, J., "African polygamy: Past and present," in: https://voxeu.org/article/african-polygamy-past-and-present (November 9, 2013).

21 http://worldfamilymap.ifstudies.org/2015/articles/world-family-indicators/family-structure.

22 Rich, A., p.230.

That this is not an accusation is primarily because it is impossible to hold anyone accountable who circumvents the conditions for accountability by abstracting themselves from the specific localizations of the bodies they inhabit. And that is exactly the point. As long as the "god trick" remains operative, their abstraction is no less prone to that of "abstract masculinity" (a term coined by Nancy Hartstock in 1983), nor to what Haraway describes as the "perverse capacity – honed to perfection in the histories of science tied to militarism, colonialism, and male supremacy – to distance the knowing subject from everyone and everything."[23]

In her critique of her own myopic vision as a younger writer and feminist, Adrienne Rich in her "struggle for accountability" explicitly names the specific, non-abstracted determinants of her particular body and the histories and conditions that inscribe it: those of "a United States citizen," "a Jew," "a feminist," "a lesbian," "a woman"; "privileged," "female," "White." The matter is not to circumvent these determinants but to name them, in order to – only then – *be able* to pose the real question: "How do we actively work to build a white Western feminist consciousness that is not simply centered on itself, that resists white circumscribing?"[24]

"Pick up again the long struggle against lofty and privileged abstraction. Perhaps this is the core of revolutionary process."[25]

References

Haraway, D. (1988), "Situated Knowledges: The Science Question in Feminism and the Privilege of Partial Perspective," *Feminist Studies*, Vol. 14, No. 3. (Autumn, 1988), pp.575-599.

Rich, A. (1984), "Notes toward a Politics of Location." Talk given at the First Summer School of Critical Semiotics, Conference on Women, Feminist Identity and Society in the 1980s, Utrecht, Holland, June 1, 1984. Retrieved from: people.unica.it/.../Adrienne-Rich-Notes-Toward-a-Politics-of-Location.pdf

Tsing, A.L. (2015), *The Mushroom at the End of the World: On the Possibility of Life in Capitalist Ruins*. New Jersey: Princeton University Press.

---

23 Haraway, D., p.581.

24 Rich, A., p.219.

25 Idem., p.213.

BIOS

Christina Grammatikopoulou (PhD) is an art theorist living in Thessaloniki. Her work focuses on art and digital technology, with a particular interest in disinformation networks, social media, and feminism. She is the founder of the Barcelona-based art magazine Interartive (interartive.org). She currently teaches Art History and Digital Culture at the Aristotle University in Thessaloniki.

Cornelia Sollfrank (PhD) is an artist, researcher, and university lecturer living in Berlin. The recurring subjects in her artistic and academic work in and about digital cultures are artistic infrastructures, new forms of (political) self-organization, authorship and intellectual property, as well as technofeminist practice and theory. She was co-founder of the women-and-technology, -Innen, and Old Boys Network collectives and currently is a research associate at the University of the Arts in Zürich, Switzerland for the project "Creating Commons." For more information, see artwarez.org

Femke Snelting develops projects at the intersection of design, feminisms, and free software. She works with and for Constant, a Brussels-based association for art and media. With co-researcher Jara Rocha she activates "Possible Bodies," a project interrogating the concrete and fictional entities of "bodies" in the context of 3D technologies. Femke currently teaches at the Piet Zwart Institute (experimental publishing, Rotterdam) and a.pass (Brussels).

hvale vale is a feminist writer, activist, practitioner of the power of erotic, and thinker @ the margins. She connects women's rights, sexual rights, and the internet poetically, politically, and practically and advocates for the #feministinternet. She discovered and learned about technology-related issues through her work, so her engagement with the internet and digital rights ranges from policy advocacy to facilitation, networking, and capacity building. Most of all, she loves co-plotting and learning from people. She does storytelling and hides in plain site.

Isabel de Sena is a Berlin-based independent curator, writer, and editor focusing on feminist approaches at the intersection of art, science, and technology. Her recent work includes publications for the Oberhausen Short Film Festival, NGbK, and DAAD Berlin, and as a curator for Martin-Gropius-Bau (Berlin), Pasadena Arts Council (Los Angeles), and Tokyo Wonder Site. Isabel is a lecturer at NODE Center for Curatorial Studies (Berlin) and, since 2016, a guest lecturer at CalArts (Los Angeles). Currently she works as a curator and exhibitions manager at FACT Liverpool.

Rebecca van Dyck is a native of Los Angeles. Since 1980 she has lived in Hannover, Germany, where she studied German literature, English linguistics, and social psychology. She works as a freelance translator and copyeditor, primarily in the area of modern and contemporary art.

Sophie Toupin is a PhD candidate in the Department of Art History and Communication Studies at McGill University, Montréal, Canada. Her current research examines the relationship between technology and anti-colonialism. She also explores the links between technology, feminism, and activism through ethnographic studies and projects. She is one of the co-founders of FemHack, a feminist hacklab in Montréal and one of the co-organizers of the TransHackFeminist Convergences. Some of her publications can be found at: https://mcgill.academia.edu/SophieToupin

Spideralex is a sociologist and holds a PhD in social economy. She is the founder of the Catalan cyberfeminist collective, Donestech, which explores the links between gender and technologies, develops action research, documentaries, and training. For the last four years, she has coordinated an international program called "The Gender and Technology Institutes" focused on privacy and security (digital, physical, psycho-social) oriented at women human rights defenders and women activists around the world. She is also the editor of two volumes exploring the panorama of technological sovereignty initiatives. She lives on the internet and sometimes can be found in her community in Catalonia.

Some of her work can be found at:
https://legacy.gitbook.com/@sobtec
https://donestech.net/
https://calafou.org/

Yvonne Volkart (PhD) is a lecturer in art and media theory at the Academy of Art and Design FHNW Basel where she also heads the research project "Ecodata – Ecomedia – Ecoaesthetics." Together with Karin Ohlenschläger (LABoral, Gijon) and Sabine Himmelsbach (HeK, Basel), she recently curated the exhibition "Eco_Visionaries. Art, Architecture and New Media After the Anthropocene." Her completed research projects include "Times of Waste." She was a member of Old Boys Network.

https://www.fhnw.ch/de/personen/yvonne-volkart
http://times-of-waste.ch

Lightning Source UK Ltd.
Milton Keynes UK
UKHW040723010421
381362UK00001B/37